Haciendas, Hammocks and Hurricanes

A house in Mexico

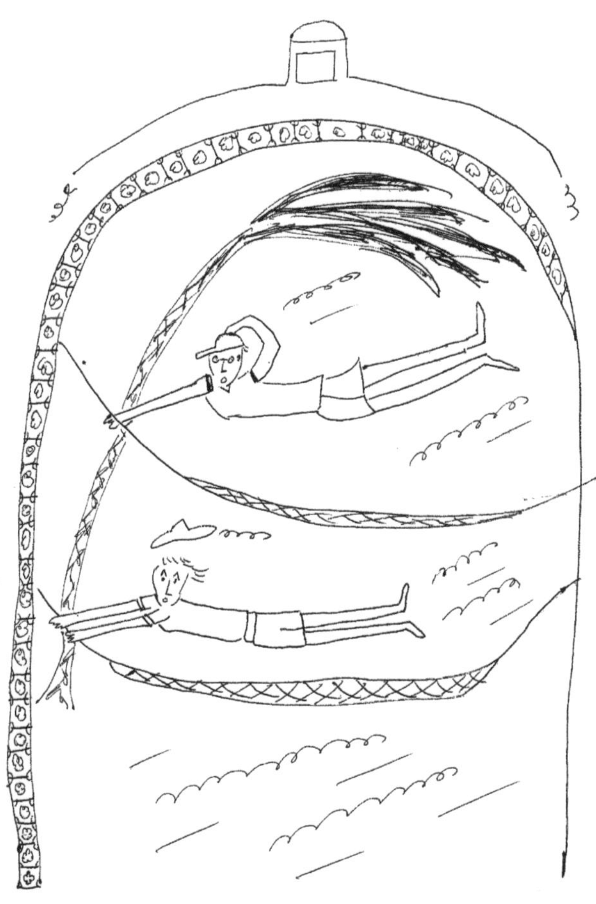

Sue Milnes

Copyright © Sue Milnes 2007

The moral right of the author has been asserted

All rights reserved.

No part of this publication may be reproduced, stored in a retrieval system, or transmitted, in any form or by any means, without the prior permission in writing of the publisher, nor shall it be lent or re-sold, hired out or otherwise circulated in any form of binding or cover other than that in which it is published and without a similar condition including this condition being imposed on the subsequent purchaser.

ISBN 978-1-84799-981-8

Contents

Introduction:
Mérida - city of ruins and dreams

'I have found the perfect wreck!'

We are sitting on the breakfast veranda of a tiny hotel tucked away in the southern Mexican city of Mérida on the Yucatán peninsula. It's only eight in the morning but the temperature has already hit the nineties and is still climbing. The fans in the roof whirr away at top speed.

Our table is shared with a retired couple. He is a Mexican who's lived in the States for many years and written books on Yucatecan architecture. They are lit up with enthusiasm.

'We're so happy,' he tells us, almost in tears, 'we have seen a pristine colonial house, right in the centre for an excellent price.'

I look at my husband Martin: what have we missed? It sounds like they have found a real bargain.

'You know, it hasn't been touched for two hundred years. It's marvellous. Nothing ruined.'

'It has a great big tree growing in the living room', his wife reminds him.

'Yes, yes, but the features are wonderful. And it has a clean title.'

Welcome to property fever, Mexican style.

Mérida is a city that for most of the year gently steams and dreams. Even in the centre where crowds jostle in the narrow streets around the market, there are peaceful squares and church courtyards where face-to-face love seats invite you to rest and, when you have finished kissing your companion, watch the world go by. Time itself has melted and stretched in the heat so that nothing seems so very urgent anymore.

The conquistadores named it after an old Roman town in Spain because when they first saw the Mayan city the limestone buildings reminded them of home. The Mexican Mérida, though, is in the tropics so that palm trees and parrots flourish even in the bustling centre. Torrential tropical downpours and the overwhelming humidity mean that many of the houses built by the Spanish conquerors and their descendents are now in a sadly dilapidated state.

Méridanos find the northern suburbs, with their swanky new houses, shopping malls and golf course far more attractive. It is crazy foreigners, captivated by the romanticism of the old colonial houses in Centro, who are buying them as local families sell up and move north.

Behind their flat, often rather drab façades, these houses have colonnaded inner courtyards crammed with fruit trees, crumbling fountains and humming birds.

Heavy doors open onto suites of tall rooms with tiled floors patterned to mimic carpets. Unfortunately they often have termites and other wildlife squatting all over the place, holes in the roof or no roof at all and old bits of machinery out the back, left over from various small businesses that have rented since the houses' glory days.

As soon as you arrive in Mérida, with its low rise streets festooned with electricity wires like permanent bunting, it's hard not to catch the bug. Great swathes of bougainvillaea spill out of hidden gardens inviting you to imagine living there, throwing open the wooden shutters in the cool of the morning, sitting in the shade by a fountain in the heat of midday and dancing to live music in one of the numerous squares after nightfall.

The clack-clack of manual typewriters from hidden offices and the thirties furniture on front porches create the feeling of a time-warp that has managed to miss the violence and unrest of other Mexican cities. In the evenings, families living in the side streets move the entire contents of their front rooms out onto the pavements to catch the breeze and sit chatting or watching the TV positioned in the open doorway.

This surreal atmosphere is incredibly seductive; it feels like you really could escape from harsh reality here. And Mérida is full of fugitives of one kind or another; escapees from cold winters, urban badlands, and messy lives. Even the toughened criminals on the run who gravitate here seem to end up running juice bars. It's like that; Mérida gets to everyone.

Just wander around and you find yourself saying: 'I don't want to leave I've got to find some way to stay'. And you are not alone. An eclectic mix of expats from all over the Americas and beyond is making its way here. Even the Guccis are rumoured to have somewhere in Centro. You may never really know who lives behind the thick shutters and the high courtyard walls although you can hear music playing and snatches of conversation as you pass by.

Local real estate agents know their target market and are wordsmiths of the first order as they talk up what is basically an old wreck while still being honest about the work involved:

- 'Wonderful old colonial haunted with unfulfilled dreams.'
- 'Speechless. This magnificent old mansion in the heart of the city will truly leave you lost for words. The house needs some TLC but…'
- 'This is the one you have been looking for all your life.'

Often the old houses have been split up among family members who partition off their share - aunty from Toluca owns a couple of bedrooms; a long-lost cousin has a claim to the kitchen. This makes some properties impossible to sell even though one of the family may hopefully have painted 'Se vende' on the side of the building.

Our breakfast partners are certainly spoilt for choice with wrecks - that day they are going to Izamal, not far from Mérida in the direction of the famous Mayan site of Chichén Itzá. Izamal is called the 'yellow city' because all the buildings in the centre are painted…yellow. Frankly this gets a little monotonous after a while, especially if you are used to the riot of pastel colours in Mérida, which is now crazily misnamed as the 'white city'.

Izamal's main claim to fame is its Franciscan convent built on the base of a Mayan pyramid, and the remains of other pyramids that loom, like ghosts from the past, behind the houses and cafés in the dusty side streets.

There is a pristine house they have heard of, just off the main square… We never found out which one they went for, maybe they are still finding it hard to choose.

This is the story of how we too fall under the spell and buy a house in

Mérida. And having taken this crazy, impetuous step we are about to find out that dreams and reality always seem to be on a collision course - especially here in Mérida, a city full of ruins and dreams.

Chapter 1: Mexico dreaming

'Monday again.'

I think the two gents standing by the train door have a competition to get this observation in first on a Monday morning.

You can see everyone else in the train carriage thinking 'Thank you so much for pointing that out to us.'

Mind you on Fridays they are always happily reminding themselves and us that it is - Friday.

I grit my teeth and tell myself 'I am going to go mad and beat up my fellow commuters if I go on with this much longer.'

Then suddenly I start seeing parrots flying around the carriage - flashes of bright red and green swooping over the grey suits, clipping laptop lids before settling on the headrests. They are looking at me with a challenge in their eyes.

'Ladies and gentlemen as you can see we have arrived at Waterloo but don't get too excited because we will have to wait for a platform to become available.'

So why doesn't he turn on the music, something up-tempo - Mariachi say - or lilting love songs from Mérida - like they do on the Mexican buses? And this is an excellent vending opportunity. Where is the guy hopping on with a tray of sweet bread rolls and vanilla-cream filled pastry cones to catch people before they make for the queues at the pricey coffee counters in Waterloo station?

An angry silence reigns in the carriage.

Flash:

We're in a taxi speeding south from Cancun airport, Mariachi music blaring. Corona bottles four foot high entice us from roadside billboards. We pass a sign for a crocodile zoo and an occasional faded board pointing down a path through the jungle to 'Cabañas' or 'R/V hook-up'.

Swinging from the taxi's rear-view mirror is a tiny shrine to the Virgin of Guadalupe with mini Mexican flags all around to form a patriotic halo. The driver, despite his nonchalant air, gives it a quick tap before starting to overtake on a blind corner. We hope anything coming the other way is an old Beetle - we've passed several already and the best of them can only do about thirty. Some look like they've been turned into convertibles with the aid of a giant can-opener.

'Ladies and gents, I apologise for the continued delay in getting you into Waterloo. I think the train ahead of us is going for the record.'

The taxi takes a left and starts bumping over potholes - the driver grabs a crucifix from the dashboard and holds it firmly against the steering wheel. 'Playa' he says through clenched teeth, 'Hurricane Gilberto.' In fact the whole place has a lackadaisical tumble-down air that may or may not have anything to do with the hurricane.

He halts underneath a sign announcing: 'Quinta Mija' outside a compound of thatched buildings. It looks vaguely like it could be a hotel.

We step out into a giant puddle up to our ankles. Martin looks around as the taxi bumps away down the road.

'Why did we come here when we could have gone to one of those motels? They're supposed to be very comfortable.'

We've been told by someone who's travelled around: 'Mexican men put their mothers and wives on a pedestal like the Virgin so they have to have a mistress for the more exotic stuff. They take them to motels on the edge of town - high walls, individual car ports with doors so no one can read your number plate, mirrored ceilings, and marble spa baths. You name it and payment by the hour. I use them all the time.'

We check in at the palapa-roofed reception desk then haul our cases past the 'shaded glade' pool - a tad green and bath-sized. Then it's bump bump bump up a spiral staircase to the second floor. The room is big and airy. But a sign in the bathroom is puzzling:

"Only natural human products down the WC please."

There's a plastic bin for everything else.

'What's a natural human product? I mean, have they got a list?' asks Martin, looking bemused and slightly worried that this holiday is going to be challenging in unexpected ways.

But ten minutes later we are floating in the turquoise sea amongst the fishing boats where the flamingos sit to dry out and rise gently up and down with the waves.

A cheer goes up around the carriage as the train starts moving. Then a groan as it stops again. A glint of sunshine strikes the carriage window for a brief second and then is gone.

Double take: there's a pyramid on the beach. This is not a Mayan ruin but a new all glass swanky beach house.

In fact, the whole thing looks like it's come out of Elle Deco.

'No way' says Martin, noticing it has caught my interest, and trying to yank me away by the straps of my swimsuit.

It's too late: I've already got the bug.

Four months later.

'Monday again.'

By now the carriage is full to bursting with parrots, and palm trees have sprung up by the WC. Hammocks slung between the doors are gently swinging to the rhythm of the train.

Unfortunately there are no delays to the service today - the scenery outside is zipping past.

There's the fresh water cenote glinting in the spring light, surrounded by lush jungle - and clouds of mosquitoes. Our first Mexican property idea hits the dust.

Look at that row of cube houses: orange, pink, aquamarine, indigo. On the edge of Vauxhall, sorry Playa. One has a 'Se vende' sign outside. Wouldn't it be nice…No don't be silly.

And right over there in the far distance, can you see the Gulf of Mexico? Lovely properties on the beach - a snip at sixty thousand dollars. No need for a/c as the wind blows all the time. And miles from anywhere. Perhaps not.

Just before we get into Waterloo on the oily Thames, can you see the turtles swimming in the lagoon? And the thatched white buildings by the water's edge - balconies at odd angles and rickety stairs from one level to another? The station sign says *Akumal* now. We're so close I can see through the window to a wall covered in ceramic suns and moons - all smiling.

By the time the train comes to a halt in Waterloo, we've bought a place on the beach. Almost.

Ticket inspection. Get your tickets and passes ready please.

'Well', says the agent looking very serious, 'first I have to tell you the bad news: foreigners can't buy property in Mexico near the border or the sea.'

Our faces fall a mile.

'But then the good news is that they can. You create a bank trust - a fideicomiso - to hold the deed so it doesn't leave the country.'

Hooray: let's have a Mexican hot chocolate in celebration - even if we have to queue.

Chapter 2: So here we are

Fast forward a couple of years.

So what's our problem now? We've got a little place on the beach haven't we? Are we getting greedy or what?

The truth is that the little place on the beach is high maintenance. It's run like a hotel with an on-site manager. This is great for overseas owners. However it also means the owners can only afford to stay there every so often.

So?

One day, the parrots and the palm trees and the hammocks have all cleared out of the train. They've had enough of the grey mornings and the dull conversation. So have I.

That night I get home and pull out a list: 'Reasons for mature gap year in Mexico':

- Great place.
- Nice and warm.
- No work.

Strangely Martin seems to have read my thoughts and produces another list: 'Reasons for not going to live in Mexico':

- Too far.
- Too hot.
- No income.

I go and cry in the bath. But I do not give up. And Martin seems to be coming around. After all, what is wrong with a year off work? Apart from the money angle that is?

We do some sums and come up with a plan:

1. Buy house in Mérida for 140 thousand dollars absolute tops.

2. Add value to the house i.e. put in a swimming pool and new bathrooms.

3. Run a Bed & Breakfast guesthouse while out there to pay for living expenses.

4. Sell at end of year for massive profit.

5. Hey presto!

6. Just as long as we don't get hung up on the plumbing.

First we have to answer various objections from friends and relatives:

- It's so far away. - Then you must come and stay.
- That country is full of bandits and drug-runners. - So there aren't any shootings in this country? Only bandits we've ever met are a double act at a filling station who claimed we'd given them a twenty not a two hundred.
- A B & B is hard work and you've never run one. - OK fair point but why not give it a go?
- What's wrong with France, Italy, Spain, and Bulgaria? - They are not very warm in winter.
- What if there's a revolution and property is seized? You'll have too many eggs in one basket. Well just look at that land-grab law in Spain. It's a risk anywhere. We might as well take an exotic risk.
- You'll be exploiting the locals. - If the locals have any sense, they'll see us coming.
- The food's too hot. Actually Yucatecan cooking is quite subtle - come and try it!

So here we are in Mérida - or rather in the countryside quite a few miles north of Mérida.

Our brief is a headache for the local real estate agents. They are used to selling ruins and call them 'fixer-uppers', like that deadly little phrase used by their colleagues in the UK: 'in need of repair'. This might give the impression they just require a coat of paint and a new bathroom and hey-presto. In reality they are likely to fall down before you have a chance to choose your paint colour.

We want something we can move straight into and with extra rooms for B & B. This leads to some creative interpretations of our requirements.

'But where's the house?'

We are in the middle of a walled compound surrounded by miles of scrubby dry terrain, parched yellow-brown by the heat. There are several small concrete buildings scattered around the enclosure in between tropical plants, open water cisterns and palm trees. It also has a huge and neglected orchard through an archway.

The count so far is two buildings with beds in them and one rough brick lean-to containing a stove and sink. A couple of other concrete sheds are heaped with junk but they 'have plenty of potential'.

So where are the living room and the rest of the house?

'Oh,' says our real estate agent, one of the growing band who have made it their mission to save colonial Mérida and the crumbling haciendas in the country around it, 'you live out in the open on this terrace'.

At that moment, we feel large drops of rain explode on our faces and have two seconds to flee back to the car before the skies deluge us with a pounding tropical downpour. The agent pulls out her mobile and frantically phones her cleaning lady shouting out:

'Angelina; hurry, hurry, the rain's coming your way, please close the windows!'

She explains that this is a constant hazard - leaving your windows open to keep the house aired in the stifling heat and then being hit by two inches of rain flooding in.

While we sit in the car waiting for the deluge to die down, she tells us she came down here from the States on spec a couple of years ago and started an agency from scratch before it became fashionable. She has a passion for rescuing old houses. We tell her we would love to take on a wreck - we're just not sure we're ready for that yet.

No sweat, we can work up to it. In the meantime, this is a good investment…

'In twenty years' time this whole area will be divided into wonderful small country estates. This' (she indicates the compound) 'is a sub-division of the land that belonged to one of the old haciendas, the great estates where they grew the sisal plant, used to make rope products, that created millionaires at the start of the twentieth century.'

'You're getting a huge amount of land for your money here.'

But not much house.

'It could be a very attractive guest complex, with just a little work.'

All the same, how will guests ever find it, bumping away down a series of tracks, after taking a country lane, having turned off a very minor road, making sure to pick the right turn out of the village - that is if they ever find the village at all?

She must be thinking: 'OK: more real estate tourists'. All the agents have warnings on their websites that they will charge for viewings outside Mérida if clients don't end up buying. They've had it with people wanting to see all the ruined haciendas miles out of town as an alternative excursion.

We get lost returning to Mérida and have to stop for directions in the local village where the twin focal points are the massive colonial church and a tall concrete water tower. Two ladies in their sixties wearing the traditional afternoon huipiles - white smock dresses with colourfully embroidered necklines - are walking past clutching coke bottles.

She addresses them very formally - courtesy is all-important here and it is considered rude to be over-familiar. The señoras smile and launch into a stream of directions.

As we drive back to Mérida, our agent tells us about Hurricane Isidore in 2002, which, unusually, came in from the Gulf of Mexico, having turned back on itself after it seemed to be heading for the southern US. It's more usual for hurricanes to make landfall on the Caribbean coast first and weaken by the time they have crossed overland to this side of the Yucatán peninsula.

But Isidore hit Mérida - only about thirty miles from the Gulf coast - hard, and lingered for two days: the electricity was off for a week and many trees were lost.

However, tropical vegetation springs back very quickly and new palm trees have been planted along the Paseo Montejo, the elegant boulevard that was built by the sisal millionaires to copy Paris, where they divided their time.

Next stop is a pink art deco house to the east of the city, about ten minutes by bus from the centre. As well as all the colonial gems, Mérida has an amazing range of art deco and modernist houses, often with their original fittings still intact.

In the wide residential roads north of the Paseo Montejo, there are many large houses that were obviously influenced by Frank Lloyd Wright with their long, low, angular lines and minimalist details. The original landscaping may have been somewhat overtaken by tropical growth, but they are still much cherished.

So this pink deco house - very sweet but it's just too far out. Still, it's fun to take a look. It has three single storey studios out the back that are rather dilapidated. However, with new shower rooms and mini kitchens they could be nice rental units. They are grouped around a half-full pool thick with algae: but not to worry, says our agent, the owners are 'sorting out the problem'.

The main house has three bedrooms, complete with the original glass louvered windows and a startling green-tiled bathroom that has two deco basins, a WC closet, a bath behind screens and a shower cubicle - so a whole household can be using it at once.

The price is very good - about sixty thousand dollars. However renters in this part of town will be students and they will have to pass through the living room to get to the studios. Also, we want to be able to walk into the centre of town ourselves. Rather sadly, we give this 'rose-pink deco cutie' the thumbs down.

Now, through the previous winter we kept our spirits up by looking at the Mérida agents' websites and dreaming. In particular we were looking at one property marketed as the 'best of both worlds'. Situated on 'ultra desirable' Avenida Reforma, and just within the Centro area, it looked like the one we wanted.

Then it went under contract and we tried to forget it. However, it has just become unexpectedly re-available. Another buyer from the UK got here before us. But their partner in the purchase, who had not travelled abroad very much and only saw it days before the final closing at the notary's, took one look and made a beeline for home.

Not too reassuring, but anyway here we are, after months of dreaming over the pictures, standing in the 'best of both worlds' with its ornate Hispanic exterior and modern interior. It is painted a vivid and cheerful yellow with bright blue and ochre tones. A plaque on the wall in elegant writing announces it is '*La Casa del Abogado*' - the lawyer's house.

It has a main house and a separate two storey building with an apartment on each floor. In between, there is a long shady archway leading into a large garden full of palm trees, with a working well. 'Just waiting for a pool', says our agent. It is surrounded by picturesque, rather crumbling stone walls for privacy.

In one of the walls there is a niche, filled with cracked tiles that must once have held a statue of the Virgin of Guadalupe - she was last seen in 1531 but in every market and bus station and outside many houses, you will still find a gilded shrine surrounded by flowers and candles.

This garden also has that rarity - real grass. As we find out just by standing there for a few minutes, there may be a reason why people don't go in for lawns here, and not just the watering. The grass is a tremendous hit with mosquitoes that rise in squadrons to do battle with any exposed flesh.

So we end up trying to listen politely while scratching - first discretely, then with total abandon - at the bites all over our arms, legs and more or less everywhere else.

The apartments need some TLC - they've been offices and don't have kitchens and the bathrooms are not exactly appealing. However the main house - partly new build and partly a much older, thick-walled building is in pretty good nick.

But after all that, we get cold feet ourselves.

- One, although Reforma might be ultra desirable, it is also highly noisy. The house is on a junction and we can hear lorries going through about six gear changes as they slow down, in case the drivers coming from the side road have forgotten the priority. They have to go all the way back up again, from first, as they speed on their way.
- Two, it is just so bloody hot in Mérida. It is hard to think straight anywhere that is not air conditioned.

We retreat to our hotel and turn on the a/c to have that think.

The hotel makes us feel like the total amateurs we are. It is an object lesson in how to do things properly and has only been open a week. The original building housed a puppet theatre and people are still knocking on the door with hopeful children in tow, asking when the next show is on.

Sofi and Dan, who own it, have spent a year of painstaking effort restoring the old building, adding a pretty two storey accommodation block in the peaceful garden and generally sweating blood and tears to create a retreat from the dust filled roads of Centro. Everything has been done properly, from a new water and sewage treatment system, to the wooden shutters and hand-stencilled decorative finishes in each room.

We decide to take a trip out of town to get away from thinking about houses for a day. There is a bus tour that leaves every day for the 'Puuc route', visiting a number of ancient Mayan sites in the Puuc hills and ending up at the best known, Uxmal.

As we sit in the tranquil nunnery quadrangle at Uxmal and watch the huge iguanas crawl lazily across the amazing three dimensional friezes, we think: this isn't so bad after all.

But when we return to Mérida in the late afternoon, we get off the air-conditioned bus, think 'Oh no; it's just too hot here', and jump on another long-distance ADO bus to get back to the Caribbean coast with its cooling breezes.

So that is the end of the Mérida dream.

Or maybe not.

It's November of the same year and we're back in Mérida in the notary's office with wads of dollars to pay the closing fees on *La Casa del Abogado.* The sellers are Venezuelan with interests in Mexico City and Miami. They moved briefly to Mérida to escape the crime and pollution of the capital. Now their plans have changed again. After the last minute withdrawal from the previous closing, they seem close to tears of relief when we sign our names.

We just hope they aren't tears of joy at having offloaded a problem on us. The signs are not looking all that great.

Usually the keys to the property are handed over at the closing but the sellers want to wait until tomorrow to check our money has arrived in their account.

There also seems to be another reason why no one wants us to go around just yet - something to do with septic tanks and digging up floors.

I look at Martin's set face as we trudge back to our hotel.

'Listen, we promised ourselves we wouldn't get hung up on plumbing. So we're not going to.'

'Right.'

At breakfast in the hotel there is an enormous buzz - everyone here seems to be searching for and buying property. A gay couple from California is closing today on a small colonial just down the street. We hear later that they do a little remodelling and sell on within six months for something like a seventy thousand dollar profit.

Work is ongoing at our house. We do not ask too many questions. In fact, we don't ask any. We are quite happy staying in the hotel.

Martin starts a diary. Opening entry: 'Why did we buy a house?'

I try to distract him from dwelling on unpleasant facts by making a list of furniture we need:

- Table and chairs (plastic).
- Fridge.
- Bed.

Too late we find we could have passed on the bed because every bedroom in the house has hooks in the wall for hammocks. In the evening, people often leave their front doors open to get the breeze and you can see the hammocks slung across the front room that becomes a bedroom by night.

However, the way to buy a hammock that is really sleep-able is to go down to one of the shops used by locals in the streets around the main market in the centre. And never pay more than twenty dollars.

But we fall into the usual trap of buying from an enthusiastic street vendor at three times that much. We notice he packs up for the day after we've handed over our cash. In fact, he probably won't need to work again for the rest of the week.

When we troop back into the hotel carrying our pricey bundle, we're greeted by a chorus:

'How much?'

'You didn't!'

'It's not big enough to sit on, let alone sleep in!'

It doesn't bode well that we can't even do a good deal on buying a hammock.

We retreat to our room to lick our wounds and then, with one not particularly practical hammock in reserve, we set out again to look for some proper furniture. Sofi and Dan direct us to a shop close by, one of a chain, called '*Casa Juanes*'. It sells furniture, beds and large white goods.

On the way, we hear an ear-splitting fanfare followed by a burst of marshal music. It sounds like a military parade is heading our way. We stand at the street corner, waiting and thinking: 'we'll never get our furniture now'. A tiny tricycle with a stripy awning peddles lazily into view. A loudspeaker is fixed precariously to the front. The guy in a white apron who is riding it presses a button and a crackly torrent of words floods the street.

We hold our ears. A lady comes out of a doorway and motions him to stop. He opens the box at the front of the trike and takes out some polystyrene cups of ice cream. Money changes hands and he is on his way with another fanfare just before turning into the next street.

'That's effective advertising for you' says Martin.

'Well you can't switch it off exactly.'

We carry on our way to *Casa Juanes.*

'I want one of those!' says Martin pointing through the window to a large orange-framed tricycle with a deep basket in front.

'Why? To sell ice cream?'

'No, to go shopping. We're not going to have a car, so we can go to the supermarket to do a big shop on that. It'll save the taxi fare to get things home.'

'You don't like shopping.'

'I will on one of those.'

'Anyway, we won't be buying much stuff at the supermarket. Let's get the bed and fridge first.'

'Well I could always set up a tricycle taxi service. Remember our trip to Celestun?'

Celestun is a great remote spot on the Gulf coast famous for its flamingo reserves and sunsets. The only problem is getting there. And the day we chose happened to be Revolution Day. For once we hired a car. Bad move. The road goes through a number of villages. In every one a big parade was underway mainly featuring the local school children performing flag waving and other patriotic activities to a thundering recording of the national anthem.

And these parades were taking place slap bang in the middle of the village - so the road was closed. We politely watched the first one - for half an hour. Martin checked his watch.

'At this rate, we'll miss the sunset.'

We tried getting around the parade in the next village. Even the tiniest place is built on a grid with a one-way system. The trick is working out which way when there are few arrows - and how do you tell who has priority when both roads are unmade and full of dogs and chickens?

Well the answer is to follow the tricycle taxis - the main form of transport. Only problem is they are not that fast and no one is in any hurry. Plus often a skinny old man is peddling away while a large lady sits up front with big bags of shopping so the pace is even slower.

We did get to Celestun in the end. I am surprised at Martin's continuing enthusiasm for tricycles though.

Armed with a pocket dictionary, we manage to stumble our way through choosing a bed and a fridge. We've already bought a plastic table and chairs at *Walmart* - dead easy as all you do is take it to the checkout. All we need now is to get the bed and fridge delivered. The assistant asks for our house number, pen poised.

We look at each other.

'344, 343, 433?' I can't remember.'

'Didn't you write it down?'

Martin tries drawing a map.

'It's on the corner, between Calle 45 and Calle 47.'

'Your number, please?'

'We'll come back!'

We troop shamefacedly out of the shop.

Flash

I'm back on the train heading for Waterloo. It's so calm and peaceful - only a little light conversation from the two soberly suited gents by the door - and all in English!

On the trudge back to the hotel, we stop another tricycle and buy a couple of hojaldras - sugared puff-pastry triangles with a layer of ham and cheese in the middle.

Fresh, these are delicious and very filling. We can't find anywhere to sit - all the love seats in Santa Lucia park are taken - so we go back to the hotel and sit by the pool in the minimalist scoop-seat deckchairs.

We feel a little guilty about eating in the hotel, especially since Dan told us that, like all the hotels in this city, they have to get the fumigators in every couple of weeks to keep down all the unwelcome wildlife that just thrives in the tropical climate. And it really is impossible to eat flaky pastry without dropping crumbs. Every time you lean over to pick up a flake of pastry, you release another one until it turns into a sort of edible snowstorm.

Will we ever get anything right? Crazy house, crazy hammock, crazy eating habits. Just as well no one back home can see all this.

Taking a deep breath, we return to *Casa Juanes*, and arrange for the bed and fridge to be delivered the following day and then take the tourist bus trip around the city.

The sides of these buses are open so you get the full benefit of any breezes but you also start to appreciate the sheer heat given off by motor vehicles. Walking down the narrow, thronged shopping streets of Centro in the hot season when it hits over 105 degrees, any passing car or bus can make the difference between gently cooking and all-out roasting.

The bus negotiates the main square - the zócalo - past the grand house of the Montejos, its ornate façade protected with netting against the birds that swarm into the central squares to roost at night. And we can't miss the cathedral - the second oldest on the continent and left refreshingly plain inside since it was sacked during the Revolution. But the real revelation is all the incredible houses in the streets north of the centre - mini French chateaux in pinks and blues, Moorish houses with cupolas and shiny patterned tiles all over their façades, more deco houses with curvy walls and wrap-around windows.

'It's like a chocolate box of fantastic houses.'

'We don't want to get carried away; this one's quite enough for the moment' says Martin.

The next morning, we are all ready to move in. We get up early, say goodbye to Dan and Sofi, promise we are definitely going to check out today, and hurry around to the real estate office to pick up the keys.

Our agent looks a little tired: she was around at our house until past midnight 'helping to clear up'. Thanking her for her efforts on our behalf, we walk the couple of blocks to our house, slowing down as we get closer.

What on earth are we going to find? Well it can't be put it off any longer.

We go through the wrought iron gate and under the archway. A long trench snakes from the ground floor apartment almost to the centre of the lawn, where there's a gaping hole. A workman is lying flat out and lifeless on the grass, a pickaxe by his side.

The delicious cooking smells (think: chicken, onion, tomato, a little light chilli) from the café next door mix with some other not so pleasant, in fact downright disgusting odours (don't think) coming from the hole in the lawn. Has the guy been overcome by noxious fumes?

As we hesitate, the workman is up again and continues the backbreaking task of bashing out the trench from the limestone bedrock that is just inches below the surface. Mexican workmen seem to prefer to use hand tools instead of power ones. It may be because hand tools are cheaper or just the way things are done. Certainly, it involves incredibly hard labour and, in this heat, breaks are essential so we can't begrudge him his little-lie-downs.

It isn't absolutely clear what is going on - the sellers are paying as they feel so embarrassed about it.

'We mustn't get too hung up with the plumbing.'

'Right,' agrees Martin holding his nose.

Things look up when the bed and fridge arrive. We half suspected our directions were so bad we would never see them again. But now we feel like we have finally moved in. We rush around to the hotel to settle our bill and check out. Do we imagine a certain air of relief that these messy eaters are finally leaving?

It's getting dark quickly and the cicadas are chirping enthusiastically in the garden - we hope they are also chomping away on the mosquitoes. The downstairs windows and doors are wrought iron and very decorative but don't fit too well. This means there are huge gaps for the mozzies to amble through and take full advantage of a new food source that is so easily available - us.

And then the water dries up.

'We don't want to get too hung up about this', says Martin, 'so let's go back to the hotel.'

I'm on the train going home from work. At this time in the evening, there's always a seat. I sit back and read the Evening Standard. Who said routine isn't good for you?

Once more in the comfort of our hotel room, we have a shower and collapse, waking up much too late to go out for a meal. Very, very carefully we unwrap a couple of squashed muffins we brought from the UK and very, very carefully eat them. But in the morning, there is a telltale line of ants marching across the floor.

'Martin what are you doing staring at the wall?'

I'm afraid the stress of our new relaxed lifestyle has get to him already.

'I'm just dealing with these ants.'

Martin thinks he's worked out a way of getting rid of them - tickle the leading ant until it gets really annoyed and decides going this way is not such a good idea, then wait for the message to pass down the line and soon they will all turn around and go somewhere else. We hope. Knowing we probably look guilty as hell, we shuffle into our chairs on the breakfast terrace.

This time we won't chance our luck by making any promises about checking out.

With a certain sinking feeling, we head back around to the house.

'We shouldn't be complaining. Think of all those TV programmes where people have the builders in for years.'

'Yes but the idea was to walk in.'

'That looks like wishful thinking in Mexico.'

However, by the evening water is restored. We rush back to the hotel and promise that we definitely won't be checking right back in again in about ten minutes' time.

Then we decide we need something to celebrate finally moving in. We have spotted a pink café one block up Reforma called - *Restaurant Reforma*, naturally. It has a cheerful look and a board on the pavement listing its specialties:

'Chiles rellenos, enchiladas, moles (verde y roja), milanesas, cocteles, tampiqueñas'.

Our stomachs rumbling in anticipation, even though we aren't quite sure what some of the dishes are, we go in through the open front door. The restaurant is in an old villa. We pass through the tiled hallway to a bright pink room full of tables with slightly worn pink tablecloths gently stirring in the breeze from the open windows. A TV is on in the corner, blaring out the Mexican version of *Countdown*, called *47 Segundos*. We can see further rooms through an archway. No one comes out.

After a couple of minutes, we venture up to the archway and start calling '¡Hola, buenas noches!'. We call and call. Nothing happens. Maybe we are too early? Perhaps we have got it all wrong and this isn't a restaurant any more and we are standing in the middle of a private house? One thing is certain - it isn't serving food at the moment.

The remains of various picnic meals sitting forlornly in the middle of our new fridge suddenly seem more tempting than when we last saw them.

We try the gas stove in our kitchen - a huge American style range with a flat plate in the middle to make, we assume, tortillas. No gas.

'No one needs hot food in this climate, anyway.'

'But they do need food', says Martin looking in the fridge at one small grotesquely misshapen bar of *Cadbury's* dairy milk chocolate that has melted at least twice and a soggy banana.

'I thought we had more stuff left than this.'

Well I think there's a grocery store just around the corner.'

'Right, let's go.'

Stumbling over the broken pavement in the dark side street, we find the tendejon in the front room of one of the old houses. And the door is open and the light on even if the shop is deserted. A hammock is gently swinging in the darkened back room.

We stand there inspecting the contents of several large glass jars on the counter. Apart from a couple of sweaty hojaldras, they are full of thick round biscuits that look like shortbread.

Martin eyes the fridge which is tantalisingly stacked with coke bottles and coughs loudly. Nothing happens.

'What are we doing wrong?' I hiss in a stage whisper.

Just then, a huge sigh comes from the back room and the hammock stops swinging. There is the thud of feet hitting the ground and the shop keeper - a middle-aged Mayan with jet black hair - emerges rubbing his eyes.

'¡Buenas noches!', he says with a certain irony in his voice.

We need to make up for this rude awakening so we start grabbing things off the shelves and piling them on the counter: bottles of coke, packets of cinnamon rolls covered in sticky icing and crisps with chilli seasoning, cheese slices and some tomato catsup - the local name for ketchup. The hojaldras look like they should have been in their hammocks hours ago so we give them a miss.

We carefully count out our money and are just about to leave when I remember something.

'Wait, we need one of those big bottles of water for drinking.'

Martin staggers back under the weight of twenty litres while I peer through the dark for hazards on the pavement in front of him.

'This is ridiculous,' says Martin lunging to deposit the huge bottle on the kitchen top before collapsing into a plastic chair.

'What is?'

'All of it.'

'We need some food.'

We sit in grim silence munching queso (cheese) and catsup rolled up in flour tortillas

A thought bubble is hanging in the air between us: 'What on earth have we done?'

It must feel like this when you've exaggerated your qualifications to get a high flying job and then suddenly realise what you've let yourself in for.

Well it is just a little too late to have second thoughts now.

We climb wearily into bed and try to sleep.

'At least there's a good chance the sun will be shining tomorrow.' I say.

'That's a good thing is it?'

Then the dogs start barking in the next door garden. More than barking, they sound like they are killing each other, very slowly and with great relish.

This is when we also find out that the new air conditioning unit in the bedroom is faulty and can only blow out warm air. Never mind, we have the ceiling fan.

After an hour, the dogs have either all massacred each other or barked themselves to sleep. Pity it doesn't have this effect on us.

We are just finally settling down when a long mournful hooting starts up, like the train in that old TV series *Casey Jones.* It comes closer and closer and then starts to go away into the distance. But there aren't any trains in the Yucatán, are there?

Once the train has gone, the dogs start again, obviously refreshed by their little nap. They carry on for another hour, and then take a short break.

Finally we doze off. Then, before six, the rush hour begins, the traffic getting noisier by the minute. And most of it seems to be really heavy lorries with pretty ropey gearboxes.

After all, this is a city, even if a small one by, say, London standards, so what do we expect?

Come the morning, we are not exactly fresh as daisies. Also, we only have two days left now to sort out some caretaking arrangements before heading back to the UK. Although we have agreed sabbaticals at work, it is going to take another three months to make arrangements for cover and do handovers.

We're put in touch with Lucia, a young Mexican woman who studied acting in New York, and has helped out a number of ex-pats. On a cost per time basis, she will sort out grass cutting, paying electricity bills and keeping an eye on things.

This sounds like such a good arrangement we get carried away and decide we want to have a swimming pool put in while we are back in the UK. Nothing daunted, Lucia asks us to make a drawing and she will get quotations.

She doesn't seem too worried when we start arranging the garden hose on the lawn, into the shape of a swimming pool, to show what we want and where.

'Oh that's no problem. It's fine.'

We get the impression that she is used to demanding and eccentric clients. And that is about as specific as we get, leaving the rest up to her.

That evening, we walk the few blocks along Calle 47 to Santa Ana square and have sopa de lima - a Yucatecan specialty with shredded chicken, tortilla and vegetables in a lime broth - at one of the stalls at the side of the market. It is delicious and filling.

Things are looking up. Even the dogs are quiet tonight.

Chapter 3: I'm lost!

It's March the following year.

As the taxi speeds into town from Mérida airport, I roll down the window to let the warm night air blow on my face.

Early this morning, Martin drove me to Gatwick through a freezing snowy blizzard. Many hours later, after a long change at Houston, I'm seriously disoriented but also incredibly elated. At last, it has really started. No more work for several months, no more cold winter, no more worries - well maybe not quite, but this is a big adventure.

It feels like I am opening the door into another world as I grope with the key in the dark entranceway. Hauling my suitcase inside, I race out to the back garden and find a switch. Suddenly, the pool is lit up against a backdrop of palm trees. I nearly jump in then and there; the water feels warm like a bath. Attracted by the light, tiny bats start swooping down to drink.

Maybe I had better wait until the morning; I've just enough energy to make up the bed and then I fall asleep to the sound of the train hooting in the background. Strange, it feels quite comforting and familiar now. My last thought is: 'I really must find out where that train goes.'

I'm here as the advance guard because Martin is still finishing off work commitments, which involve a trip out to Japan - another in a long series that at least means we have a large number of air miles to get us to and from Mérida via Miami or Houston. The alternative is to get seats on charters to Cancun and then take the bus (four and a half hours and you get to see two videos one of which will usually be *Garfield* dubbed into Spanish).

Lucia - between houses of her own and wanting a garden for her daughter - had been going to live in our house until we arrived, while she was supervising our works. Then, having installed her furniture, the noise and dust from the pool excavation were just too much, so she moved in with her mother.

However she needs somewhere to store her furniture, and we are only too happy to keep it in our house as it means we now have, among other things, a huge old rocking chair, an ornately carved wooden chest of drawers and matching mirror, a bright blue kitchen dresser and an ironing board.

One day we know that Lucia will want all these back. In the meantime we're very grateful for the free loan. And the rocking chair makes us feel we have joined Méridano society. Almost every porch, however small, has a set of rocking chairs arranged invitingly in the shade, with a low table to the side just waiting for cool drinks.

The next morning, I wake at first light, excitement overcoming jet lag. I get out my UK mobile and phone Martin to give him a running commentary on the pool as I look down at it from the bedroom window.

'Hi, the sun is shining, the sky is blue… Yes there's water in it. No, it's all under control.'

'How's the garden?'

'Well to be honest, there isn't much left. But don't worry, I'm working on it.'

All Martin has seen is some photos Lucia sent us of a vast gaping hole with a JCB stuck in the middle of it, and piles of excavated rock piled around the bald garden that had lost all its grass. At that point, we were incredibly glad we had decided not to be there when the pool was being excavated. What the neighbours must have thought is another matter, with days of drilling through solid limestone.

The next pictures Lucia sent us showed a workman standing in the empty pool, smoothing off the concrete sides. We decided to go for concrete as tiling would have been pretty expensive and also likely to need more maintenance. In total the pool, including all the work and a filtration system, cost around eight thousand dollars - amazing compared with UK prices, and absolutely no need for heating. Well, except maybe for three weeks in January when the outside temperature can drop to sixty - at night.

Now, I say to myself, I am going to be very organised from the start. I pull out my old laptop and fiddle with the screen until it comes on. We've already agreed to keep spreadsheets for all capital and ongoing costs plus a mini plan for all the works. I also have a little list:

Things to experience in Mexico, culled from various real, rough and independent guides:

- Dramatic scenery.
- Vibrant architecture.
- Vivid colours.
- Incredible contrasts.
- Fantastic customs.
- Real Mexican food.
- Genuine culture.
- Everyday life.
- The beauty of it all.

In the meantime, I need to get to grips with the pool before it turns green.

Lucia comes around later that first morning with the specialist who built the pool to explain how the filter and vacuum works and how to use pool chemicals. Somehow, either we miss out a stage or the jet lag is beginning to tell, and I struggle for the next five weeks trying to make the underwater vacuum behave itself, getting increasingly desperate. I hold it above a tiny twig, pleading:

'Go on, you know you can do this.'

So much for encouragement; it just will not suck up anything. Dyson this is not. In the end I resort to using a sort of giant fishing net to scoop debris off the bottom, with really unimpressive results. Only when Martin arrives and we ask for another demo, does a little light come on - ah so you need to close *that* valve. At least I only once come close to gassing myself with chlorine.

Lucia is incredibly proud of the pool; it's her 'baby'. She went through all the tortuous stages of its construction, and now other clients want pools. There's a steady stream of prospective pool owners coming around in the next few weeks to see it.

One rather sniffy guy comes and stands with his arms folded and looks down his nose at the water lapping against the concrete sides. Then he very pointedly tells me:

'I've just been to see an absolutely wonderful house. It has an exquisite mosaic pool - just perfect.'

Meaning ours is just… concrete. 'Yah boo'. I'm about to find out that one-upmanship is alive and well in the world of Mérida fixer-uppers.

After standing in the direct sun while we do the pool briefing, then standing some more in the apartments as I discuss further work with Lucia, I start feeling very faint. Earlier this morning, I crazily quick-walked ten blocks to *Walmart* - as it's the only supermarket I know how to find - to get some shopping. Now the room is beginning to swim around me. I sit down on the concrete floor with a thump.

'Quick,' says Lucia, 'you must lie down.' She helps me into the front room of the house where an old mattress is making do as a couch.

'Stay here and don't move at all, I'll be back in a moment.' Lucia's training as an actress in New York means she knows how to make you listen. So I lie there and wait thinking:

'Great start. Day one and I've already lost the plot.'

In a moment Lucia's back with a bottle of regular coke, that trusty medicine. I drink it straight down and feel better immediately. Lucia is obviously used to clients who are not only demanding and eccentric but who have also temporarily forgotten they are in Mexico where it is ninety-six in the shade and closer to the equator than Egypt. She pats me on the head:

'Be sensible, OK? I'll come back later to see how you are.'

So the first lesson is: don't overdo it. Quite a nice lesson really, if it means lying in a hammock with a cool drink to hand for about three hours every afternoon. Not that I seem to have much time for siestas in the next few weeks. I'm determined to make sure as much of the work as possible is completed before Martin arrives.

And what is more, my parents Sheila and Roy are due out here in four days' time to keep me company. I've managed to convince them that Mexico is really very civilized. The minute they see this house and garden they are going to be persuaded otherwise unless I do something quickly. I decide to make a tour to assess the damage.

Vibrant architecture? No I can't tick that one just yet.

First impressions count. You come off the street through a rusty gate into a rubbish-strewn courtyard flanked by flowerbeds full of the Mexican equivalent of bindweed. The JCB has obviously hit the side of the archway on its way to the pool - a big gash reveals that the building once went through a distinctly purple patch. What should be a great view through the archway to the oasis of the back garden is now a scene of devastation.

The trouble is the garden has been all but destroyed by the excavation for the pool. The palm trees rise up out of dust and bare rock. In an effort to restore the lawn, we've already ordered a lorry-load of turf, which is not very sensibly due to arrive at the start of the dry season.

And when the turf is eventually laid after a number of delays, it is in ragged, random strips with large gaps between them. My parents, life-long gardeners, take one look at it and say nothing. I'm then condemned to watering it three times a day in the searing heat.

When Martin arrives several weeks later, his first comment is:

'I don't see why you had to water it so much, it looks fine to me.'

Little does he know.

On the left hand side of the front courtyard, the ironwork steps up to the top apartment have almost disappeared under convolvulus. I push my way through and find I am covered in giant hairy orange caterpillars. In other circumstances they would be quite cute. Right now, I am not in the mood for starting a petting zoo.

Amazing wildlife? No, caterpillars don't count.

The top apartment, when you manage to get up there, is not even halfway ready for taking paying guests. In fact calling these places apartments is somewhat overstating the case, and then some.

Both apartments have two rooms. The idea is to make the first room in each into a kitchen/diner (meaning: let's get out of doing breakfasts if we possibly can).

We decided that the kitchens should be built totally out of yellow concrete, with the surfaces polished smooth.

Mexicans are very skilled in creative concreting, using a special type that comes with the colour ready-mixed in. Just say the word and you can have concrete sofas, concrete bed bases, concrete tables and benches. In fact, you could have a house completely furnished in vivid concrete - long lasting and impervious to termites.

Over the winter, Lucia made a start, finding us a local Mayan builder - Señor K - whose company has done work for many expats. They've put in a kitchen work surface along the back of each room, including concrete sinks and holes for stove tops. I stand there trying to convince myself that the minimalist approach is going to work.

We need to add a stove top, a fridge, a pull down table. Money, money, money. And the shower room in the top apartment is going to eat more of it. The door opens straight onto the loo so you scramble over the pan to get into the room.

Coloured bathroom suites are very big in Mexico. Retro fans have a field day. Bright sunny colours I can definitely live with. But here the basin and WC are a particularly nauseating public lavatory green. 'If it ain't broke, don't fix it' is generally our motto - not this time.

Vivid colours - half a tick

At least the bedroom has a very high ceiling and is bright and airy. The only problem being that the big space means the noise of traffic from the street gets magnified into a rumbling echo. Plus the floor is tiled in a pattern that's best summed up as 'aqua seasick'. The blue and white pattern swirls around like a choppy sea and anyone looking at it for more than a minute is definitely going to start feeling nauseous. Still, it can be covered in rugs that will also soften the echoes.

Now I regret our decision not to put in a balcony and spiral stairs at the back so that the apartment has direct access to the garden. It will be a nice touch. Oh well, I will just have to get covered in caterpillars again.

The downstairs apartment is dark. Never mind - it will be cool and has a marble tiled floor in the main room and a big long window you can hop through into the garden.

Then I realise that the little room - called a bodega here – which we have added at the back (to house the hot water boiler for the apartments) has a completely glassed door - the only outlet being the window into the shower room. Our guests will be asphyxiated. That glass will have to come off. At least the shower room is all white and will be fine for the moment. However, there is just one little problem.

The bathrooms have lethal-looking contraptions coiled around the shower head and plugged into sockets only inches away. These heat the water as it passes through, and are supposed to be economic and effective, but we can't rent the apartments when the bathrooms look like they've been rigged up as death traps. Guests will think they have blundered into the Mexican equivalent of the *Bates Motel.*

Somehow, we'd forgotten about these when asking for hot water to be piped to the kitchens.

So the workmen are back again and start gouging out channels for piping with their pickaxes. This is a favourite occupation. One American lady we meet later is having a new house built and has had a really hard time persuading the builders that they should put in ducting for the pipe work and wiring as they build up, not hack it all out once the walls are in place.

Out in the back garden, I count ten palm trees including four different types - some with long, drifting foliage that reaches right to the ground, others with sharp, shiny green fronds that stretch for the sky before gently dipping at the ends. Some have a fruit that looks like dates - on investigation I find it's mainly stone and not for eating.

I report back to Martin, who loves bananas:

'I don't think any of them produce edible fruit. Sorry, you won't be able to wander out and pick a banana or a coconut. But don't worry; they've got plenty in the market.'

The archway connects the apartment building with the main house. On the ground floor here, there is one long space. The iron and glass double front door opens straight into the main room. To one side, a staircase with a wrought iron balustrade climbs to the first floor. On the other side, big double doors open to the archway. One step up leads to the dining area and, right at the end, the kitchen with a door onto the garden. The main room can't exactly be described as cosy as it has so many exits and entrances. At least the thick walls keep it cool.

'Maybe we can turn the archway into a lofty living room?'

'Not just yet.' I can sense the anxiety in Martin's voice, even on a different continent. 'Don't get carried away.'

Beyond the kitchen, but only accessible from the garden, there is another good sized room - originally for a live-in maid - off a utility area with a loo and shower. It could make an excellent guest suite once it's been cleaned and repainted.

Upstairs, the front bedroom has a pearly pink shower room. In the next bedroom there are floor to ceiling windows that open straight out into empty space. The big bedroom at the back has a walk in closet leading to a bathroom with a huge dark blue tub.

Yup, there's plenty of potential here even if not much else right now.

'Martin, I think we should get rid of the bath and create two nice shower rooms. Also, it will be great to have a balcony running around the whole of the first floor overlooking the garden. Plus we really need a patio around the pool. That will only cost 140 dollars.'

'You can do the patio; nothing else 'til I get there, OK?'

Phew, that ploy worked. I've got the patio. And I've already decided it's going to be done in warm orange concrete. The builders come in a team and do the whole thing in a day, working very fast to smooth the different layers before they dry out in the baking sun.

Vivid colours - one tick.

That afternoon, feeling revived, I decide to check out the local shops. Right next door, there's a tiny internet café. In Mérida, to run a cyber joint, you should be male, about twenty, act nonchalant and play super-cool music -

definitely not Mariachi but something more like the Reggaeton hit *Gasolina* though even this has a trumpet voluntary every few bars just to add an extra something.

This internet café comes in handy when I realise after only a couple of days that I've spent my four hundred dollar credit limit on my UK mobile phone. It goes straight in the cupboard and everything international is strictly by email until we have broadband installed and cotton onto cheap international calls over the internet.

Lucia takes me down to the *TelMex* office to set up a phone contract and they are due to come and install the phone 'within a week'. I make sure I am in every morning. No show. They'll definitely be around on Friday. I wait in all day. No one turns up.

Then I read on the local bulletin board that three months is a very short wait as far as *TelMex* goes.

Now this may just be a Mexican urban myth, but apparently one popular way around this is to find a *TelMex* van on the street, wait for the engineers to return and then 'persuade' them to come along to your house and put in the phone. It's said that some people even get into the vans and refuse to leave until their phone is fixed.

Fantastic customs? Not sure if I can tick for this yet.

It certainly seems like so many people are using their powers of persuasion that the engineers never get around to their official list of calls. I need a phone pretty quickly for local calls so I go out and buy a *Telcel* pay-as-you-go mobile. For forty dollars, this is a pretty good deal. I decide to put off using any persuasion with *TelMex* engineers until Martin arrives, in case they get the wrong idea.

Next to the internet café is a real café, the source of the very appetizing cooking smells that waft over the back wall. Somehow I am off to a bad start with the owners after getting annoyed by the amount of rubbish that passes over our front railing, tossed there by the students who go to and fro the café from the university just across the road.

Lucia goes into the café to ask them politely if they could put out an extra rubbish bin.

'No, they already have one for their customers and it's the snack bar on the corner anyway.' Oh dear. I've antagonized the neighbours already. I'm very tempted to put out a big bin myself with a sarcastic message on it. Except I'm struggling to think of a snappy put down in English let alone Spanish:

'Missed again! The bin's here, stupid.'

Why not appeal to their better instincts instead:

'The world is your living room. Don't trash it.' Somehow, I can hear the laughs already.

Anyway, if we put out an extra bin, we will have to pay for even more rubbish to be taken away. Lucia explains that Mexicans don't necessarily see themselves as litter louts:

'You know, they think they are helping the local economy by keeping the street sweepers in jobs.'

Well that is certainly one way of looking at it. And the wiry sweeper is very accommodating - he offers to do our courtyard for 50 pesos a day. This is five dollars - a quarter of our daily budget. No way - not for less than five minutes' work. Maybe those natty shades he is wearing were not just found in the trash?

We head downtown to set up a contract for refuse collection. The office is rumoured to be along an alley just off the zócalo and up some stairs into a building with open air corridors that has not had a refurbishment since the fifties. Apart that is from the installation of a/c. We stop every few doors to enquire where the refuse office is - and a blast of icy air hits us before the door is hurriedly closed.

Eventually we squash into a tiny room where a large lady in the standard working wear of white short sleeved blouse and black skirt is having a heated conversation with a young couple. After about twenty minutes, looking defeated, they get up to leave.

'Right what do you want?'

Lucia explains.

'Oh no, you can't do that here. Ring this number and a collector will come around to your house every month to take your payment.'

Lucia phones up. He'll be around before 11 on Friday. There's something about Fridays. A year later he still hasn't been around, although the trash is collected once a week, every week. Maybe they think it belongs to the café next door? Well in a manner of speaking, they're right.

Now what about some local food? It's a big cop-out to keep on going to *Walmart*.

Around the corner, there's a tortilleria where rough grained corn tortillas cost about seven pesos for a kilo. Some people still make them at home but many use the tortillerias in all the markets and in many side streets in central Mérida and you don't have to go too far to find one. They have a conveyer belt with the dough being fed in one end and the cooked tortillas collected up at the other.

Tortillas are one of the staples here along with refried beans and are best eaten very fresh (you see people going twice a day to get them like the French go for their baguettes). After that, they get tough and have to be deep fried and turned into taco chips.

There was a picture in the local paper recently of an enterprising vendor who had laid out her stale tortillas all over a sunny pavement to crisp them up. I just hope she checked the pavement first.

That first day, all on my own, I proudly purchase half a kilo, neatly wrapped up in a paper parcel, and this is quite enough for lunch, dinner and well, OK, I give up by breakfast. And I have to confess that - feeling like the wimp I am - after that I go and buy a packet of the larger, white flour tortillas from the local grocery store as they stay fresh longer even if they aren't half as wholesome. Softie gringa.

Real Mexican food - half a tick

At least I have the right change for once.

In fact having the right coins is a big problem - it seems like there must be little gnomes somewhere who hoard all the small change in Mexico. If you go into a corner shop or buy something from a street vendor, anything that requires more change than about ten pesos is going to cause an insuperable problem. But how do you get hold of enough change in the first place?

On the Caribbean coast, you can get away with using dollar bills for tips and to make up change, but in Mérida the dollar is not so readily accepted as an alternative currency. So you start hoarding five and ten peso coins yourself, and praying that the ATM won't give you a 500 peso ($50) note, which is a total nightmare to get anyone to accept - even supermarket cashiers don't like them - unless you happen to spend it all in one go, which, when your daily budget is 200 pesos for everything, is not likely.

I also find two bakeries within walking distance and work out that I need to take a tray and pair of tongs, make a selection, and then go to the till when I have everything I want.

Here there's quite a range of pan dulce - sweet bread - some in the shape of shells with a stylized sugary pattern on the top. If you're lucky, you may get a small amount of jam, chocolate or some nuts inside but they still look rather boring and dry and need to be dunked in hot chocolate to pep them up. There's also something that's a cross between bread-and-butter pudding and cheesecake - and tastes like it as well. I don't dare go in the pool for several hours after eating it in case I sink.

Real Mexican food - fat tick

Most of the markets in Mérida are covered - on the outside are all the little loncheria counters with chairs and tables and fierce competition for customers. In Santa Ana, there is a parilla (grill) doing superior seafood and steaks, still for an amazingly low price. Another stall is just a large glass box filled with every bit of chicken you can imagine and then some.

You indicate which piece you want and then it is manhandled onto a tortilla with pickles added. There is also a row of stalls selling all the condiments and sauces you could need for Yucatecan cooking.

One of the stallholders entices me to try a small sample of his liqueur and then ticks me off in very good English:

'It's only two o'clock and you are drinking!'

The stuff is not bad and somehow I'm persuaded to buy two jars of a fruit called nance preserved in the liqueur. Needless to say, the liqueur in the jars makes the sample seem positively silky. Plus nance turns out to be something like a large yellow olive with a huge stone, not the luscious mini apricot I had assumed it was.

It's worth another tick for Real Mexican food though.

Around the market, people are talking Mayan with rapid, short words. At least I think it is Mayan - not that I'm exactly fluent in Spanish to know the difference.

The Mayan language is more widely spoken than Spanish in rural areas in the Yucatán and the TV news is repeated in Mayan. Every day, one sees faces in the street that have the same features - including the distinctive curved nose - as the carved heads at the ancient Mayan sites.

There is pride in the Mayan heritage throughout the Yucatán; however there is also some prejudice against people who are obviously of pure Mayan descent.

Advertisements on TV and in magazines are pretty blatant - the models, especially children, look almost European. However, many Mayan beliefs and traditions have managed to survive by merging with Catholic festivals - the Day of the Dead is just one of them.

Something else that has survived is the love of tiny dogs. Before the conquistadores arrived, the Mayans never used dogs for hunting, and just kept them for pets - or, it is rumoured, to eat. People still like to have decorative small dogs like miniature poodles or chihuahuas, but they don't eat them anymore.

'No', I reassure Martin, 'the cheap chicken is definitely chicken.' I hope. Poor guy, he is really wondering what he's coming out to here.

A few blocks up the road, I find a shop called '*K'chorros doggie spa*' where two assistants are hard at work grooming and clipping while a long line of dog containers show how much work they have. The pampered pooches waiting in their cosy cages are the lucky ones.

A vast number of decidedly ungroomed semi-wild mongrels wander around all the villages and even in the city. Animal charities have their work cut out trying to keep the population under control.

You always get worried if a dog starts following you - it may have decided that you look like nice people and are ideal for adoption. Mostly in Mérida, though, it is so hot the dogs only have energy for lying in the shade - and barking at night, like the ones next door. We won't mind if anyone eats *them.*

A little further up the road, on a prominent corner, is the plaza de toros. It's not clear if any bull fights still take place here. Huge posters advertising pop concerts in other venues plaster the exterior. I pass an open window and see two women hard at work typing on old machines. Double doors reveal a wide area at the back of the arena. Better not venture inside in case there are any bulls around. Ernest Hemingway I am not and I don't care if I am missing out on a tick for genuine culture.

Even further up the road, there's a theatre specializing in regional culture and shows in Mayan. The play on at the moment features a famous local comic – Cholo, real name Héctor Herrera, who is pictured on the posters with a fierce-looking lady. Well I'd rather them than blood and guts in the arena.

That's far enough for one day. I head home and take a dip in the pool. Now this ain't bad at all.

With so much work going on at the house, the following afternoon I decide to get out for a few hours. It seems like a curious choice, but I take a bus going north to find a French supermarket called *Carrefour.*

The whole point of the trip to *Carrefour* is really in the hope they have Belgian chocolate bars. I'm already getting chocolate withdrawal symptoms and like any addict, I'm on the hunt for my next fix.

This is not going to get me any ticks for Real Mexican food - except this is where chocolate came from originally…

I've already found that *Hershey's* bars from the States are fairly widely available - at a cost - but this is not the same as Belgian chocolate or even *Cadbury's* dairy milk. And locally made chocolate bars seem to have something added to stop them melting - they are very brittle.

First I have to get there.

A good way to get to know a place, as I am just about to find out, is to get lost on a bus, preferably the totally wrong bus as well.

In Mérida, there are not only a myriad of different bus companies but also minivans - colectivos - that ply all the popular routes and have alarming doors that suddenly swing wide open as the driver stops to pick up someone waiting at a street corner.

All the buses have a list of stops on their route painted on one side of the windscreen. Although there are some bus stops marked with a 'Parada' sign, the colectivos all seem to stop fairly randomly as well so the best bet is to find someone else who looks like they are waiting and join the queue. It is also a good idea to tell the driver where you want to get off (there is a flat fare) to be sure they will stop.

Of course, I don't do this.

The bus driver has a pop music radio channel on and Shakira is keeping everyone entertained.

'Hey', I think, 'here I am on a bus in Mexico, the sun is shining and I don't have to go to work for months. This really isn't bad.'

So my mind isn't totally on the route.

We head north through the city and pass a huge shopping complex and still there is no sign of *Carrefour*. I'm sure it must be here somewhere.

The bus joins a motorway. We pass a big shop called - *Liverpool*. I do a double take then remember reading somewhere this is the swankiest department store in Mérida. Interesting choice of name.

The bus turns off the motorway into a big industrial estate. It makes a stop at a huge *Coca-Cola* office and depot and then comes out and rejoins the motorway. I have come out of my daze and am starting to get worried. We seem to be heading away from town.

The bus turns off along rural roads. We are in a village outside Mérida. Click, click; whirr, whirr. We must have passed *Carrefour*. So how come I haven't seen the sign?

The bus stops in front of an old hacienda that has been turned into a hotel and restaurant. Maybe I should get off and take a look around? Maybe not - with my luck, this will be a once a week bus and I could be stuck here.

There is great merriment on the bus when the driver politely asks me where I am going and I blurt out:

'*Carrefour*.'

I kind of get the gist of his reply:

'*Carrefour*? *Carrefour*! That was six miles back. How could you miss *Carrefour*?'

A kind lady in the seat opposite indicates she will let me know when we get there.

So I pay another four and a half pesos to go all the way back again. Everyone on the bus shouts out:

'*Carrefour*!' when we get there.

But how strange; it doesn't have a sign. Only later do I find out that it was taken over just the day before, and is now the supermarket-previously-known-as-*Carrefour*. They need to change all the bus windscreens. At least I haven't been totally stupid.

This area north of Mérida feels like an American suburb. The shopping mall may be called 'Gran Plaza', but it has a long line of American eateries like *TGI Friday's*, *McDonald's* and *Pizza Hut* and very European style swanky shops and hair salons with prices to match. This is probably due to the influence of Cancun.

Apparently, there was consternation in Mérida when a branch of *Zara* opened in Gran Plaza - previously it has been muchísimo snob to wear the label as it showed you could afford to go to Cancun for shopping trips. A big percentage of the money in Mérida comes from Cancun - people who own hotels and restaurants there although they prefer to live in Mérida.

But after all that, the chocolate is so pricey I can't bring myself to buy it. With some trepidation, I get back on a bus, making sure it is going into town.

Local forms of transport - gold star.

The best part of that trip is actually getting to see the train that has hooted its way through my dreams for the last two nights. As the bus heads back into town, there it is, making a stately progress up the central reservation.

And it really is like the train from '*Casey Jones*'. So, maybe it is not a steam train but it has a massive great engine with the driver way up in a tiny cab, like a picture from a children's book. And behind the engine - not the long vintage '*Orient Express*' train on its way to a romantic destination that I imagined, but just two dingy freight containers.

The reason for the hooting is obvious - it runs along an unprotected track and frequently has to cross the roads that cut through it. It must be an absolute nightmare to drive the train, looking out for pedestrians, cyclists and dogs as well as cars.

And now I realise where it must be heading: the port of Progreso on the coast, about thirty minutes' drive north of Mérida. Here the Gulf is so shallow that the actual port is something like six kilometres out to sea. So there is a truly surreal pier stretching into the far distance - it looks like one of those architectural details in the background of a Dalí painting - to take the freight to and from the port.

Somehow I manage to get off the bus within five blocks of home. I'm in bed fast asleep by eight o'clock, dreaming of endless piers with steam trains running along them.

Everyday life - big tick.

Chapter 4: Lizard poo and all that

I am beginning to get the feeling I am not alone in the house. Every so often, there is a strange noise; something like:

'Chac chac chac chac-chac-chac-chac.'

It seems to follow me around. I begin to wonder if the place is haunted by an ancient Mayan spirit, remembering there is a Mayan rain god called 'Chac-Mool.'

However, this spirit leaves small black droppings that look like commas.

Then I spot the culprit. Ha! It is a gecko or lizard about four inches long. In fact a whole colony of lizards is living inside the house, each with its own territory - behind the air conditioning units and around the window frames seem to be the prime spots as far as lizard real estate goes.

These guys are certainly regular; once I start looking, I realise there is lizard poo all over the house. I am just glad that the big iguanas that I can see crawling over the garden walls haven't found their way inside. Their poo is a lot larger.

And their favourite spot for doing number twos seems to be on the concrete surround of the pool. Well at least it isn't in the pool. Correction: Theirs isn't but something else's is. Eventually I work out this is probably a bat that sleeps in the palm overhanging the pool. Well it is great that our first visitors feel really comfortable and settled in.

Iguanas - the big daddies of lizards - are not exactly lookers. They have scaly skins and jagged ruffs rising along their backs to their beady-eyed angular heads. Most of the time, they haul themselves around like they have zero energy. This is a big act.

That afternoon, I am just having a rest out in the garden when suddenly - bump - something falls out of the tree behind me. I see a blur of greeny-grey skin rush across the bare earth and scrabble up the jagged stone wall.

'Ha, I saw you!' I shout out. The iguana freezes, pretending it is part of the wall. The only give away is an eyelid very slowly lowering. I do not take kindly to being winked at by this creature with bad personal habits.

'And in future, find somewhere else to do your business.'

Amazing wildlife - tick. Maybe change amazing to disgusting, or at least challenging.

I can't rest for long. I have only one day to get ready before my parents arrive. There is just time for a quick sweep and mop and then I have to jump on the long-distance bus over to Cancun to meet them. At least they will have a bed - that is about all. No wonder, then, that I decide it is a good idea to extend our stay over in Akumal.

My parents are keen to go and look at Playa del Carmen, although I warn them it has grown so much it is now a city. We take the colectivo up Highway 307.

'Ah,' says the driver seeing my father's mane of white hair as we clamber on board: 'El Presidente' and offers him the prized front seat.

'And what about the President's wife?' asks my mother under her breath as we squeeze ourselves into the back row of the minivan.

Playa is certainly busy these days. The development stretches for miles along the Highway.

'It's a big place' comments my mother as we pass superstores, a huge electricity plant, furniture depots and car showrooms.

It is hardly recognizable from the first time we'd been there, but I want to show my parents the charming *Quinta Mija* hotel, where we'd first stayed.

My parents head to the beach to find a café while I hunt up and down. The *100% Natural* restaurant with its shady courtyards and terraces is still there so where is the hotel?

Then I realise with a shock that the new shopping street going off Fifth Avenue is right where the hotel had been. I look closer - then make out a couple of the old hotel buildings with their outside staircases, now experiencing a new life as offices and retail units. That is all that is left of the once tranquil and hippyish little hotel.

Feeling quite sad, I go to rejoin my parents.

A dispute is underway. My father wants to try a piña colada.

'Roy it's only ten thirty in the morning,' protests my mother.

Now my father is no boozer, but he does like to try the local tipple when on holiday, and is very determined to get his way. He calls a passing waiter and asks for a couple of coffees - and then quickly adds his own order.

'Well I hope we don't have to carry you back.'

'No, no,' assures my father. Then the waiter arrives with a huge glass full of a whitish rich-looking liquid and a wide straw. My father takes one sip. His sun hat nearly blows off.

'Phew'.

We make it back and have a very long siesta that afternoon.

Next day, we decide to postpone going over to Mérida again, and instead take the colectivo the other way down to Tulum.

Everyone has seen the pictures of the ruined Mayan city at Tulum, perched on a cliff, its white buildings reflected in a dazzling turquoise sea. I remember the huge posters on the London underground tantalizing frazzled commuters, myself included, before we bought our apartment in Akumal. Maybe that's what did it.

Since the last time I was there with Martin, the site has been spruced up with a posh visitor entrance and on the seaside, a new wooden viewing platform and a stairway winding its way down the cliff to a bathing beach far below.

It must have been really startling, when the Yucatán coast was mainly jungle, to round the corner in a boat and suddenly see the ruins. In fact, the sea route was the only way to get down this coast well into the twentieth century.

When we arrive at the site entrance, there is a tourist train waiting to carry visitors the half a mile or so to the site proper.

'No, no,' declare my parents, when I suggest we could take it. 'We're fine to walk.' It is a very hot road though; everyone is walking single file so as to stay in the shade from the trees at the side. The train toots past when we are halfway along. Its passengers look as cool as daisies. Maybe it is not such a bad idea after all.

The site is pretty busy even though it's not huge and has nothing to compare with the pyramids at Chichén Itzá. But as ever; location, location, location really counts. The aquamarine backdrop of the sea is stunning and makes you feel cool even if you aren't.

We wait patiently to see the famous relief of a 'diving god' who is shown falling head-first to earth, his feather headdress somehow still holding on. The sun is very bright and the crowds are pressing around us, so we convince ourselves we can make it out and retreat to the shade.

'I'm thinking we could use a picture of that god for 'no diving' signs around the pool.'

'Then it had better be a little more visible than the original.'

After doing the site we sit in the shade and watch two large scaly iguanas play tag around us. My mother opens her bag to get out a handkerchief and they immediately abandon their game to approach us.

'I think they're expecting food. I bet people feed them all the time.'

'They look quite fat enough,' says my mother, closing her bag very firmly.

'Now would you like to take the train back?'

'Yes please.'

Amazing architecture - plenty of ticks. Then again - do the big tourist sites count, if you're supposed to be doing the rough independent thing? Whatever, it's still amazing.

But new guests are arriving to stay in the flat in Akumal tomorrow, and we have to leave for Mérida.

So it is on the bus for the four and a half hour journey.

Local transport - more ticks.

'Not very scenic, is it?' comments my father.

'No, mainly scrub and jungle,' I admit. I think they have visions of deserts full of cacti and rocky outcrops interspersed with colourful towns buzzing with fiestas. But the interior of the Yucatán peninsular is well - sleepy and still mostly scrub and forest. The bus calls in at Valladolid, a smallish colonial town that is - well asleep and we only have ten minutes so there is no time to get out of the bus station and explore.

Dramatic scenery - no ticks.

We arrive in Mérida in the late afternoon and take a taxi to the house. I cross my fingers that nothing disastrous has happened whilst I've been away. Everything seems OK and we all take a dip in the pool to cool off.

That evening, we stroll down to Santiago square. Here there's a café called *La Flor de Santiago* with echoing tiled floors and high ceilings from which descend big twirling fans on long stalks. Altogether it's another place that has the feeling of being unchanged since the fifties.

We decide to order some of the local Yucatecan specialties: panuchos and salbutes - kind of open sandwiches with a small crispy fried tortilla as a base, piled with shredded marinated chicken, red onion, lettuce and avocado - the only difference is that the panuchos have a layer of refried beans inside the tortilla. We also order omelettes with chaya - our guidebook describes it as a kind of 'super spinach'.

Now for drink. You can have *Sol* or *Corona* if you must, however, there are some better beers - *Superior* (of course), *Dos Equis, Bohemia.*

'These Mexican snacks are really very filling', comments my mother.

'Which is good news - we'll need to watch the pennies while we're out here.'

'On this evidence, you'll have no trouble. Our whole bill is only eight dollars including drinks. We paid more for the coffee in Playa, and even then we had to ask for milk.'

Real Mexican food - big tick

So far so good. I've put my parents in the back bedroom so they won't get disturbed by the traffic noise. We all turn in for an early night after our long journey.

Next morning though, I come down and my parents are already up and have started weeding the garden.

'Hope you slept well?'

'Hmm', says my mother pausing with the trowel in her hand. 'These Mexican politicians certainly like to talk and talk and talk.'

I am feeling a little puzzled. Have they been out again later on and wandered into some political convention?

My father indicates the wide balcony of the pretty pink house that sits beyond the back wall of the garden. I've noticed PRD painted in big letters across the front wall on the side street.

The PRD (Party for Democratic Revolution) is the main left of centre political party in Mexico and is in power in some cities although the President comes from PAN (Party for National Action), a centre-right party.

'They were out on the balcony having discussions most of the night', says my father. 'Maybe it's just a convention and not like that all year.'

'I hope we don't stir them to revolution with our private swimming pool and all that.' I say, feeling nervous. We've been warned to keep very clear of Mexican politics - they love big discussions and political rallies and endless in-party feuds but they hate non-Mexicans getting involved - in fact, the Constitution prohibits it.

'And I'm hoping they don't go on like that again tonight,' says my mother with a sigh. 'I think we're going to need long siestas here in Mérida and not just because it's hot.'

In the evening, we are all getting ready to turn in. My mother is in the pink shower in the front room. I am tidying up downstairs. Suddenly I hear a commotion from upstairs.

I rush up and call out: 'What's happened?'

My mother's voice comes from behind the shower curtain, sounding slightly frothy:

'There's no water. And I am covered in soap.'

I run around trying all the taps. No water at all.

'I can go and get a bucket from the pool?' I offer.

'Don't worry I'll make do!'

In the middle of the night, there is a great gurgling from the roof as the tank refills. It almost drowns out the noise of the PRD discussions.

Next morning, the water runs out pretty quickly. It is time to call in the builders again. They scramble over the roof and poke about in the front courtyard. The conclusion is that the municipal water pressure is insufficient to reach the tank on the roof.

Suffice it to say that the money my parents have given me to buy 'a few little decorative touches and some treats' all goes on a new water tank at ground level, and a pump to get the water to the roof tank.

My parents are pretty relieved to get back on the bus to finish their holiday with a few quiet days in Akumal, on the Caribbean coast.

'So how do you like Mérida?'

'Very interesting, but it will be nice to get back to the sea.'

As soon as they leave, the political convention is over. Peace and quiet reign and the only disturbance after that, from the PRD's house, is the soft thud of very ripe mangoes falling to the ground from their tree.

Now I am under strict rules that I am not to buy any more furniture until Martin comes out, sun loungers excepted. However, when I see there is a 'garage sale' on at the Mérida English Library, I decide I will go along.

The library - known as MEL - financed by donations and subscriptions and mainly staffed by volunteers, is a favourite meeting place for English-speaking expats from the US and Canada. A kind of colony has grown up around it - the owners' names on the plaques outside houses in the same street are more Anglo than Hispanic.

And big advantage - the MEL twice yearly garage sale is conducted in English. It's kind of cheating, but then I have only been in Mérida for a couple of weeks. The sale is popular with locals as well as expats, as it is known that people departing after their winter stay just want to offload stuff, and there are bargains to be had. The concept of boot sales and flea markets is not very well developed in Mérida - people tend to keep and repair things - so any kind of second-hand sale is still a novelty.

The MEL patio is heaving when I arrive, and makes the Harrods sale look like a genteel tea party.

I don't recognize a single plant on the busy garden stall, and decide to go for the one that looks most like a cactus - this is Mexico, after all - with a bunch of long curling arms like a big insect feeling its way out of the soil. It is only later we find out that it produces large flower pods that open to look like pieces of torn, rotting flesh.

Amazing wildlife - gory red tick.

Getting caught up in the buying frenzy, I snap up five plastic wine glasses in assorted colours, telling myself they will make good decorations as the word on Mexican wine is not encouraging.

I also try really hard to buy a fifties pink mirror, also in plastic, with a curlicue frame - fantastically retro - for five pesos (about 50 cents) until I realise that the box of junk in which it is sitting is someone else's haul. After that, I have to get out of there quite fast.

Now, having acquired all these essential items, I feel I am pretty much ready for Martin's arrival. The patio is completed. I have more or less bribed a taxi driver to cram some sun loungers into his cab and now they are temptingly arranged by the pool. The apartments just need to be furnished and we can get going on the B & B.

All ready and then, just before he is due, it starts to go hideously wrong.

Chapter 5: What on earth is going on?

So I think there isn't anything left that could possibly go wrong with the plumbing? Ha, ha.

Two nights before Martin and my mother-in-law Pauline, who is coming for a holiday, are due to arrive I carry out my regular evening check around the place. I glance into the shower room in the downstairs apartment. All is fine - no wait a moment - that is black water coming up the drain. Black water as in the technical term meaning - raw sewage. Unfortunately, not something you can close the door on and hope it goes away.

I have a sleepless night and phone Lucia first thing the next morning.

'Lucia, I've got another emergency. Yes I know. They just keep on happening. This one is really desperate. Please can you phone the builder? Thank you. Thank you.'

Fortunately he has someone free, and they came and have a look. I am hoping it is just a blocked pipe, but no, it's worse than that.

Apparently, the main septic tank does not have a drainage well. Water will normally drain away through the well, leaving only the solids that will gradually decompose over time. The septic tank should only need emptying once a year or less, as long as you are careful to put only your natural human products down the WC. That is the theory. Obviously it has gone wrong here. Surely I can't have gone to the loo that much?

A well is needed quickly. The builders locate a drilling rig and say it will be delivered at nine sharp tomorrow - the day of Martin's arrival. Meanwhile, the top of the septic tank is left off to allow some liquid to evaporate, and I decide not to flush the toilet until the problem has been sorted. Fortunately, I get constipation from sheer embarrassment.

I send Martin an email saying 'Can't wait 'til you get here - everything's fine,' and cross my fingers.

But I am still crossing my fingers and everything else crossable at five the following afternoon. The drilling rig has been 'unavoidably delayed' at the previous site (they must have even worse problems than me, but by now I'm not in a state to feel that sympathetic). The crew turn up just as the sun is setting. Five hours to go before Martin and Pauline arrive - and I just know there will be no delays, they will sail out of the airport and be at the house earlier than expected.

I turn on all the lights, as darkness descends very quickly in the tropics and it is night by the time they get the drill in place. Then the drilling starts and I get a taste of the torture the neighbours must have gone through whilst the pool was being excavated. The limestone bedrock is only a couple of inches below the surface and the vibrations come straight up through the floors and walls. Clouds of dust blow everywhere. Every time the drilling stops, I think they have finished, but they are just pausing to change the drill bit.

This is when I learn that you should always have a good supply of chilled *Coke* in stock, as plain water does not get a very good reception with people working through their evening.

At nine pm, I ask how much longer, trying not to sound too rude. They will be out within an hour. Phew, it is still possible that Martin and Pauline will never know. Ten minutes later, there is a knock on the front door.

'What on earth is going on?', demands Martin looking more than wild after twenty hours of travelling.

Just at that moment, the drilling stops for the final time. I breathe a sigh of relief.

'It's all under control', I say, 'come in and sit down and I'll explain everything later.'

I try to ignore the team of workmen dismantling their rig in the background and carrying it out to the lorry on the road.

'Tomorrow you'll be able to admire the beauty of it all Pauline, I promise.'

The next morning we are all taking a tour around the garden. Under an old stone bench, we notice a drain cover.

'I wonder what's down here?' muses Martin, tugging at the concrete cover.

I groan: 'I think I know.'

And guess what is under it - yes a deep drainage well that looks like it has been there for years. It must have been cut off from the septic tank by the recent work to sort out the bad smell in the lower apartment. Talk about ironic.

'I think I'm going to cry,' I announce.

Now we really do hope that our plumbing problems are over, but we are obviously hopeless optimists. The next moment we step inside the lower apartment and the bad smell is back worse than ever. They do say that after about five minutes, your sense of smell wears off and you don't really notice a bad pong. But we know that any paying guests will not be in there five minutes to test this theory. They will be straight out the door long before that.

It is all too much so we decide, as it is a Saturday night, to go along a few blocks to the southern end of the Paseo Montejo to watch the free weekly variety show called '*Noche Mexicana*'.

Now you might think that this kind of entertainment is put on mainly for the benefit of tourists - you will be totally wrong. Tourists can come along if they want to, but they had better be there early to get good seats - or any at all. All the free entertainments in Mérida - and there are several every week - are wildly popular with the locals. There are different acts from all over the country at *Noche Mexicana*, and most of them are excellent.

Tonight there is a very large jolly girl acting as compère - apparently she is a presenter on the local radio station. She repeatedly reminds us of the generosity of the sponsors, *Corona* beer - well it has to be them, or *Sol*. Plus, we are to remember that there will be 'presents' later on. This causes much excitement in the audience.

The evening starts with solo 'ranchero' singers - male and female dressed in kind of high class cowboy and girl gear - black with white detail. People start singing along and they descend into the audience to pick duet partners.

'Oh no,' groans Martin, 'they're coming this way.'

'It's your chance for stardom.'

'I don't know the words.'

'Just say "mi corazon" a lot.'

'No way, I'm going to check the food stalls.'

He shoots off, just as the flamboyant lady singer changes direction and picks out an old gent, who is very happy to sing along with her about his aching heart.

Martin doesn't return until he is sure the coast is clear.

'They have chips, but there's a terrible queue. Hey, what are you eating?'

'A very nice man came along with a bag of peanuts and asked us if we wanted to try them,' says Pauline.

'So after that, we felt we had to buy some.'

'They're very tasty. Don't worry; we got a bag for you too.'

Next on is a fantastic dance troop, the women in full silk dresses - each one a different colour - that billow out over their lace petticoats, the men very cool in white suits, shoes and hats. They dance so fast and furiously that our photos come out as a rainbow-coloured streak.

And then the long-anticipated sponsor spot - three disco dancers who make the dancing at most weddings look quite professional. They are really terrible. Maybe they're a scratch team? We hope so.

The audience seems ready to overlook the hideous dancing - amazing for a place where everyone can move pretty well - because they know they will soon start lobbing freebies into the crowd.

First come the plastic tumblers, done with a sort of *Full Monty* tease - plenty of feinting and twirling around before they finally come flying through the air.

'Quick, quick, catch one Martin!', urges Pauline, getting into the spirit of things.

This is when we realise why all the front seats are occupied by locals an hour or more before the evening starts. You are definitely in with a better chance at the front. And boy, can some of the regulars reach high and wide. They would be amazing in goal.

Next up are baseball caps. More twirling, coquetry and pretending to throw but stopping at the last moment. Ha, they are giving people at the back a chance. Right, if they aim at the same spot on this side, we might be lucky. We ready ourselves; the cap comes winging its way towards us. Snap. It's gone. Wow, the Méridanos are usually so courteous and polite. Here, the gloves are off. In fact it is war.

Last on the list of freebies are beach balls. For these, you must dance. The *Corona* team descends into the audience. You do a kind of shake and twist right to the ground and back up. Even grandmothers are willing to get on down for a beach ball.

'Catch me doing that!' says Pauline.

'I'm going to look at the craft stalls.' announces Martin in a big hurry, zipping out of his chair.

'We'll come with you.' we chorus.

After this great set, the crowd starts thinning out but the show is not over - bring on the marimba players. They stand in a semi circle and really go for it on instruments that are related to xylophones. One guy doesn't even need to look down and he has the most complicated part. The music has a rhythmic, lilting quality, almost like calypso. This is more like it.

It follows us down the road as we reluctantly head home, jet lag beginning to tell for some of the party. We feel happy and relaxed, sure we can sort out any small plumbing problems. What are we worrying about?

And we've earned big ticks for:

- *Vivid colours.*
- *Incredible contrasts.*
- *Fantastic customs.*
- *Real Mexican food.*
- *Genuine culture.*

We've relaxed too soon. The following day we are on a visit to a cluttered furniture store when Pauline is cut by a piece of jagged wood that is sticking out of a bed, slicing into a surface vein.

'Hey, where's all that blood coming from?' queries Martin.

Pauline hasn't felt a thing and the trail of blood leads half way back around the shop. The owner helps patch things up, and we get a taxi home quickly. We don't realise how bad the cut is and just put a bandage on it.

Our showers seems to be bad places for visiting relatives - the next morning Pauline's leg suddenly erupts in a huge explosion of blood *Psycho*-like all over the walls.

This does not count as a tick for vivid colours.

Dredging up our half-remembered first aid courses, we get her lying down on the floor and hold her leg up as high as possible, the bathmat pressed against the cut. Pauline is the only person who seems perfectly calm.

'Martin, you're looking very pale. Is it the blood?'

We are in total panic - how do you call an ambulance in Mérida? I try phoning the tourist police, who speak English, but they can only tell me about pharmacies.

Help!

Then I phone our new Spanish teacher, Jaime, with whom we've just signed up, and he immediately gets an ambulance for us and then comes around to help interpret. We really owe that guy.

I get in the ambulance with Pauline. Martin says he will stay and clear up, so we don't come back to see a vivid reminder. This is true heroism from someone who really doesn't like the sight of blood.

Now one thing you really need to take with you to hospital here is not medical records, not personal details - no, just money. Instinctively, I must have grabbed my bag.

The ambulance takes us to the *Centro Medico de las Americas*, not too far away, behind the Paseo Montejo. An orderly brings a wheelchair and Pauline is seen almost immediately by a casualty doctor. Not bad compared with the NHS. I begin to understand why Mérida is quite a centre for health tourists from the States who come down to have operations at a lower cost than they could back home, and often with better care.

We then have to wait to see a specialist. Now I really wish I'd taken an intensive Spanish course when I arrived in Mérida. The specialist has little English to match my poco Spanish.

'Much blood with wood in shop'

'I'm fine, really. Just need a good bandage, I should think.'

'You must no move.'

'Goes on airplane, two weeks, is OK?'

'Yes, OK. But use this cream.'

He writes out a prescription. Wow. No wonder people go to the *Doctor Simi* pharmacies, that promise only low cost generic medicines manufactured in Mexico, not expensive imports. The NHS has got something going for it after all. This prescription costs something like 60 dollars for a small tube of cream.

We wheel back into his outer office where a secretary is watching TV. Her sole job seems to be to write out the bills, which have to be paid before we can leave the office. Just as well I have my bag with me as I don't know what happens if you can't pay - we would probably have to phone Martin to bail us out, or we'd still be there days later.

Unfortunately, the cream doesn't seem to help too much, probably because it is so hot, and it all happens again a few days later, just as we have ordered pizza for supper.

'Now don't worry about me,' says Pauline, 'and stop panicking. We'll have our food first then go to the hospital. I can eat pizza with my leg in the air.'

Old first aid courses flash through my mind: Patient must not eat or drink until a doctor has given the all clear. Seek help immediately for bad cuts etc. etc. But the patient is sitting quite cheerfully on a cushion with her leg up on the coffee table. And the Haiwana pizza is just arriving from *Vito Corleone's*. So we sit down and eat it, then head for the hospital in a hire car we've picked up that day, ready for all the sightseeing trips we are going to take with Pauline.

A different casualty doctor this time advises keeping the cut dry - no cream. I am sent off to the hospital cashier to pay for a new bandage. I am the only one with any money on me. Stupidly, I haven't checked my purse. I tip out everything I have and count it out. An impatient queue, brandishing their credit cards, waits behind me.

'Three peso coins'

'Five fifty centavos bits.'

'Nine ten centavos coins and a stray dime.'

Not enough: I need ten pesos. I troop back along the shiny corridors to the casualty room.

Never mind: the doctor asks me for all my change and adds the missing amount from his own purse. We thank him profusely - junior doctors don't get paid all that much, so it is very kind of him.

He also makes out a prescription for antibiotics to take to a pharmacy later. They do the trick but Pauline really has to keep her leg still so we can't go on any excursions.

And then it gets super hot. I mean 106 degrees, and rising every day for more than a week. The kind of heat where walking upstairs leaves you bathed in sweat and you feel light-headed after just a few steps down the street. It is like a heavy, suffocating duvet that you can't throw off.

And this is the dry season - April - with no chance of any rain to give some respite.

There is a/c in the bedrooms but not downstairs and we don't want to run it all the time as it uses so much electricity. So we tough it out with fans, dips in the pool (not such a penance really, although this is out of bounds for Pauline) and ice creams. At least our house has thick walls so the front room is less hot - even if every so often, a pungent reminder of the problem in the lower apartment seeps in on the heavy air. We are postponing further investigation to save Pauline any more traumas.

We have *Rumicub* tournaments and whist drives. And we are so hot, we can't face cooking. So lunch every day is cheese, tortillas and tomato salad. Or tuna, tortillas and tomato salad just for a change, with crisps for some salt.

'So what delicious Mexican food did you try on your holiday Pauline?'

'Oh mainly tuna with a pizza every so often.'

Only the tortillas get a small tick.

The one thing that really keeps us amused is the bird activity on our lawn. A troop of medium sized black birds is hard at work pulling up every strand of dried grass to make their nests. Thanks guys: that's really smartened things up.

But then the vultures appear, watching and waiting patiently for the chicks to hatch out. They sit on the old windmill in the garden next door, absolutely still. Every so often, the black birds launch a defensive raid. Parental instinct overcoming fear of the much bigger birds, they swoop low and actually peck at the vultures. The vultures don't bat an eyelid. It seems they just can't feel a thing. We cheer all the same, every time the smaller birds go in for the attack.

Amazing wildlife - a tick for the brave black birds and a big cross for the vultures.

I have never seen anyone look as relieved as Pauline when we take her to Mérida airport for her return flight. Lovely cool Britannia here I come! Not one for the album somehow, this holiday.

However, we have at least managed to locate something Pauline is very keen to find: little animals made up entirely of tiny beads sewn tightly together. She bought some on a previous trip to Guatemala and promised to take more back for a friend who is writing a book on Central American textiles and handicrafts.

Just by chance, before disaster struck, we'd been into a shop in Centro that sold items from Chiapas, the Mexican state located south of the Yucatán and bordering Guatemala. We noticed the shop was displaying t-shirts with images of the masked 'Sub-Commandante Marcos', the educated, clever and elusive leader of the Zapatistas who have been fighting with the government for rights for the local indigenous population in Chiapas. In a glass cabinet, there's a whole menagerie of beaded animals all in vivid colours.

Hummingbird?

Oh yes, I'll have one of those.

Shrimp, parrot?

Definitely!

Ant, turtle, lizard, dolphin…

We proceed to buy up something like half the stock, carried away trying to get an example of each one. Not only that, we also buy beaded collars, tiny bags to hang around the neck and bracelets.

Then I spot a heap of stuffed toys made from rough hairy wool: Cats, llamas, frogs. These will be good presents for young nieces and nephews. Yes please. I'll take a green cat and an orange one, yes and a blue frog…

Mission accomplished: at least something has gone right for a change. And when we get back in the early morning after taking Pauline to the airport, at six thirty am it is actually just about cool enough to sit out in the garden for breakfast.

'Hey', whispers Martin, 'what on earth is that?'

He is pointing to the grassy slope beyond the pool.

'Looks like an anteater or something'

A dark hairy *thing* is picking its way through the dewy grass on high, delicate legs. It has a longish snout and an even longer hairless tale.

Suddenly, it is gone. We rush indoors to look it up on the internet.

'Was that it? No, it isn't an anteater. It has a rat-like tail, not a bushy one.'

'This is the one. It looked just like that. An opossum.'

'Strange creature, strange name but kind of sweet. I wonder if it lives in our garden?'

'Shouldn't think so, not enough cover.'

'Do you think we could tame it?'

'Don't even try.'

Amazing wildlife - gold star.

Chapter 6: Waiting for a call

'Go on, I dare you'

We have spotted a *TelMex* van parked in a road just around the corner from our house. Loitering on the shady side of the street, we are trying to psych ourselves up to approach the engineer on his return and 'persuade' him to come home with us.

Martin is still doing some work remotely, and we are getting desperate for a phone line and internet access at home. The local internet cafés have become like homes from home. I've told Martin that the only way to speed up installation is to find an engineer and use inducements to get him to come and fix the line.

'Is this wise do you think?' asks Martin, looking edgy.

While waiting in the electricity office, we've seen a TV advert encouraging people to denounce bribery - showing a teacher taking money from a pupil in exchange for passing them in their exam, then another pupil going around the school with a megaphone telling everyone. But…we can't see how else you can get a telephone installed.

So we are all ready to pounce on the guy - and then he doesn't come back. Well it is lunch time and maybe the siesta hour or perhaps someone else has pounced first. Whatever, we are just getting too hot standing around and head for home. Somehow, I don't think we could have bribed him - I mean, how do you know what's the going rate? Knowing our luck, we would probably have got arrested and been featured in the next anti-bribery ad.

Anyway, we might legitimately be next on his list for today. We stay in all afternoon. Well maybe tomorrow then. Soon every morning at breakfast we are intoning:

'Today's the day *TelMex* will turn up. Yes, believe it!'

Lucia keeps phoning them for us and relays their promise that they will definitely, without fail, have our phone installed by Friday. Well that certainly sounds more definite than 'mañana' which generally means 'wait and see, and then wait some more.' Fridays come and go. Obviously this is a new euphemism to understand; 'definitely by Friday' meaning 'that gives us more time before you complain.'

In the meantime, someone recommends we get cable connected instead. We take out a contract with *Cablemas* and three days later we have broadband internet and cable TV up and running.

Immediately we get hooked on *TreceTV* - the local channel. It's very local, which means that nothing outside Yucatán state ever gets reported - except hurricanes. We sit glued every evening even though we can only understand one word in ten. The ditty is very catching and easy to learn Trey-Cey-Tey-Vey. We are making progress.

The state Governor - Patricio Patrón Laviada is an extremely tall man and towers over all his constituents. He has the lead slot on every bulletin. And he's busy - always opening this or visiting that. In between there are ads trying to persuade country people to give up the feral way of life - meaning using the local cenote for bathing and for other things as well - and have a WC and shower installed with a grant. Then a guy comes on and goes through all the news again in Mayan.

Genuine culture - possible tick?

We are also hooked on the local daily paper - *El Diario de Yucatán.* Our favourite item is the naming and shaming pothole spot - every day the photographer is sent out to take a picture of a hole in the road or other hazard, like an overgrown hedge or broken pavement, somewhere in Mérida. We just hope the trees at the front of our courtyard don't grow any more or we'll be in there any day soon.

Four months later, we give up expecting *TelMex* to call and go down to the office in Centro to cancel our contract and get our deposit back. We don't rate our chances. But like lambs, they hand it all back, every peso. However it involves waiting in three different queues for most of the morning. Somehow, we get the impression that we aren't the first.

One problem solved. Just a few to go.

The pong in the lower apartment is now so bad that you are in danger of keeling over if you stay in there too long. There is no way we can start thinking of lettings until we have got it sorted.

Maybe there is a dead iguana or something stuck in the drain pipe? Señor K's guys came around and do some exploratory digging. Nothing there, all clear. Lovely fresh air for one day. An even worse pong is back the next. What is the problem? This is getting ridiculous. It's like someone doesn't want us to get our B & B going.

We suddenly remember the tearful state of the previous owners when we signed the contract. Maybe the house is cursed with a problem that no one can solve like a kind of malodorous poltergeist. Cue pictures of endless excavations, drillings, re-plumbing, septic tank replacements going on for years and years. Do we need a shaman to cleanse the spirits from the house instead of a plumber fiddling around with the piping?

Then Martin has a simple idea. What about a new U-bend on the downstairs shower? If this is broken, there will be no water seal so of course the gases from the septic tank will get through. A no-brainer really. Señor K's guys come around again and install a new U-bend. No pong for one day. No pong the next day or the next. Hooray. The bad smell is exorcised at last.

But wait a moment, now there is smelly water oozing up from the floor in the downstairs apartment kitchen. We haven't used the apartments at all. Where on earth is this coming from?

I venture over there that night to retrieve a mop. Five large cockroaches sliver and click their way down around the sides of a manhole cover in the floor. This has not been obvious by day because it is covered with the same tiles as the rest of the room. What is down there?

Another mini septic tank, apparently. So how many of these wretched things are there? Well at least three. We've found another one in the front courtyard after sweeping away months of accumulated leaf mould and litter.

Time to call in the specialists: the men who come by night and do unspeakable things under cover of darkness. The head guy has silvery hair and is treated with great respect by his work gang. They open up a deckchair and cover him with a blanket. He sips something steaming from a silver flask while clutching a mobile in the other hand. Business is good. Meanwhile his team gets to work - with buckets.

We stand at the window.

'I thought they were going to pump it out.'

'So did I.'

'Those guys deserve their money.'

Local customs - tick (with major caveats).

At least now we will be starting with - how can we put it - a clean conscience?

So that's all sorted then.

Oh really, are we never going to learn?

Well one thing we certainly need to learn is Spanish.

I never studied Spanish at school and had just one term of weekly lunchtime classes before I arrived. I am just about alright on numbers and that is it. Martin didn't even have time for that.

It is through one of the MEL members - Sally - that I've found our Spanish teacher, Jaime. Sally fell for Jaime soon after arriving in Mérida and they've moved in together. Jaime is a graduate but has to supplement his income with teaching in the evenings.

Three times a week Martin and I walk over to the shared house they rent, one road behind the Paseo Montejo. The owners need extra money and live in just one of the rooms. Everyone shares the kitchen at the back of the house. Another room is rented by six waiters working in a taco bar on the Paseo. At night, they all sling their hammocks. They don't earn much, so this arrangement maximises the amount of money they can send home to their families in villages some way from Mérida.

Jaime is incredibly enthusiastic, and we sit at the kitchen table and pretend to buy the saucepans and everything else to hand.

Martin stands behind the table and acts as the shopkeeper, and I am the customer, and then we change round.

'¡Buenos días!'

'¡Buenos días! ¿Habla usted ingles?'

'Hey that's not allowed.' Jaime protests. 'You must speak Spanish. You can't ask if they speak English!'

'Er, right. ¿Tiene un … er what's the word for frying pan? Right, er un sartén, por favor?' Always a good move to add 'por favor' on the end - meaning: please, please understand what I'm trying to say even if it makes a two year old sound like a genius.

'Si.' Martin brandishes the frying pan, looking pleased with himself.

'¿Cuanto cuesta?'

Martin looks puzzled.

I mouth: 'How much?'

'OK. Right.'

'No English!'

'OK. Esta bien. Ha.' Martin looks at his watch. 'Son las ocho en punto.'

'No, no: ¿cuanto cuesta el sartén? Not: ¿que hora es?'

'OK. Dos mil pesos.'

'You have got to be joking. Two thousand pesos - that's what ... two hundred dollars or something.'

Jaime leaps up and pounds the table.

'No English or I will make you do stem changing verbs right now!'

As Sally says, Jaime should have been on TV. He is so enthusiastic and animated. But life is life: he worked for one of the big drinks companies after graduating until he got sick of the competitiveness, and left to get more into the Mayan culture and approach to life. But his day job - conducting marketing surveys - doesn't pay much. He explains that most graduates have to do two jobs to make ends meet. After a few weeks, Jaime gets better paid work in Cancun. At least by then we have got quite good at buying things *in Spanish*, especially kitchenware.

It is quite a relief to get out of the house because the problems just seem to be piling up.

The right-hand wall at the back of the house looks like it is about to fall into the pool and the hurricane season is fast approaching.

On the other side of the wall is a large and decrepit colonial mansion. It has an imposing portico and some style even if its turquoise paint is bleached-out and its masonry is falling away in great chunks. This is one ageing grande dame in need of TLC as the real estate agents say.

Every so often a skinny guy comes around with a bucket to our gate and asks for some water as the tank has packed up next door. We get the impression that he is some kind of informal caretaker because the house doesn't seem to be lived in by the owners - well we hope not, given its state.

The hopes of getting the wall repaired by our neighbours look slim, so Señor K's guys are back again, feeling really at home by now, to stick the wall back together and paint it a bright orange - well, why not? We notice Señor K is so busy he needs a brace of mobiles to manage his business.

Shortly afterwards, there is unusual activity next door. Huge rolls of old matting, rusted oil drums, a rotten wooden wrangle, tattered mattresses and large pieces of ancient machinery that look like manual printing presses are appearing under the portico on a daily basis. A big clean-up is obviously under way. And boy, must that house be in a mess. New rubbish is piled high every night for more than a week.

Then one day a 'Se vende' sign appears on the wall, with a mobile number to call. The owner is obviously looking to cash in on the growing market for 'fixer-uppers'. I am intrigued and angling for a chance to look around it.

'I don't think it's a good idea,' says Martin very firmly. 'What if they think you want to buy it?'

'Well maybe we do.'

'Absolutely no way. We've got enough on our plate with this house and it's in good condition. Anyway, we don't have the money.'

'Well there's no harm in looking.'

That afternoon, I notice a couple sweeping up and doing a final clean. I ask if I can look around. No problem. Great: I'm in.

There's a grand piano in the entrance hall underneath an enormous chandelier. This place was really something, once upon a time. It is single storey with high-ceilinged rooms, one opening into the next around a long central courtyard with a parrot in mosaic on the tiled floor, echoed by a giant glazed parrot on the wall on either side. Intriguing.

The kitchen and laundry - backing onto our repaired wall - look like they haven't been touched for half a century or more - the appliances are so old they are almost antiques. No wonder our wall has been in such a state. I just hope someone buys the place soon, as it looks like everything that can leak does.

At the far end of the courtyard, there is a building big enough to be a separate apartment, but it is still crammed with machinery despite the clear-out. It must have been used as a workshop at some point. I can only get into one of the four bedrooms off the courtyard (maybe they are hiding literal skeletons in the closets in the others; it feels like that kind of place). There is a bathroom that looks like it had a partial makeover in the fifties. The elegant glass-panelled doors have evidently been under attack from termites for years.

Vibrant architecture - faded raggedy tick.

It is crying out for rescue. I phone up the number to see how much it is - 245 thousand US dollars if you treat direct with the owners. Real estate agents here charge a hefty commission of about seven per cent of the selling price, payable by the seller, but realistically they are the conduit to the people in the market for properties like this.

Anyway, dream on: like Martin says, we have enough problems on our side of the wall. Just as long as someone doesn't open up a boutique hotel, to compete with our B & B, right next door.

We had better get a move on with fitting out our apartments. Our thinking now is that we will aim at the longer term visitor. Mérida is a favourite destination for 'snowbirds': retired or semi-retired North Americans who escape here to avoid the worst of the winter back home.

They like to rent small properties in Centro or out at the beach in the little coastal villages either side of Progreso. Some buy up what the agents call 'credit card' or 'pocket money' houses in the centre - two room tiny places costing maybe thirty to fifty thousand dollars with perhaps a small yard at the back, that can be left in the summer, and are cheap to keep going. They tend though to drive hard bargains when renting to minimise their outgoings.

The other problem is that the snowbirds have all flown back to their native lands with the onset of the hot, dry season and will not be returning until after the hurricane season is over in early December. We have got things back to front. Well, we're not relying on an income just yet from doing rentals; it is just that we can't stay out here more than a year without some money coming in. So our idea is to have a soft launch, testing the market to see if we get any bookings for the winter and what kind of income we can expect.

We need to get going on furnishings, so that we can take pictures and set up a website. The summer will give us time to sort out other issues, like any licences we will need, what taxes are due and how they can be paid, and any thing else that has to be sorted out. We hope it isn't going to be a long list, and we know we are in the dark about how to go about some of these things.

However, we've been told that the notary can handle many of these issues. After all, as long as you keep square with the tax man, and don't have more than six guests at any time, setting up and running a B & B in the UK isn't that complicated. Maybe it is different here?

We turn for some advice to a Mexican who has been in the tourism business for many years, recommended by someone who says he will know the pros and cons.

He is a small, neat man who first off tells us we should understand that he is a natural pessimist. Oh well, it sounds like he will be realistic. We do a tour of the apartments and the garden. Then we sit down and have a talk.

'You see, there are some problems in Centro. There is a kind of hotel war breaking out. The owners of the traditional hotels are getting real annoyed with all these foreigners doing up the old colonial mansions and opening boutique hotels, taking their business.'

Now, we have wandered into the foyer of one of these once imposing hotels, right in the centre, and it really looks like it has lost the plot - a couple of tatty sun loungers sitting forlornly in a leaking central courtyard with broken flooring; not exactly welcoming.

As we couldn't even find the reception desk we aren't surprised if they are losing out to the bijou, design-led newcomers. What it means is that any new operation has to make sure it is set up properly, with necessary licences and so on, otherwise it will be vulnerable to being shopped to the taxman by the competition.

'What you could do is go up market and try for visitors staying a few days. You could offer them a luxurious and relaxing retreat on the edge of Centro.'

We look at each other, knowing that the noise from the road outside starts at six in the morning. This will be a drawback to going big on ambience. Never mind, we have plans to do something about this.

Renting out long term to locals - with limited use of the garden and pool - is an alternative although people will not want to pay more than about five hundred dollars a month. The best bet, as we think, might be to look for longer stay visitors willing to pay more given we are within walking distance to Centro, the English Library and the Paseo Montejo. Plus the very private and quiet garden and pool are selling points. Our pool is bigger than those in many of the smaller hotels - some of them are just for 'dipping'.

So we now have some food for thought. We thank him for his realistic advice. Seeing that our faces have got longer and longer as we talk, he tells us not to be too down hearted. The best thing is probably just to try it out and see what happens. Plus he reminds us that he is a dreadful pessimist and, with a wave, is gone.

So now our number one priority is to fix the road noise problem. We have an idea that will also do something about the rubbish that is still coming over the front fence at the rate of about one crisp bag every fifteen minutes.

One morning, we hear very loud music coming from the pavement just outside. I go to take a look and can hardly squeeze out of the gate due to a giant inflatable crisp bag sitting right in front of it. I feel like I am in one of those children's books where things suddenly grow enormous overnight.

But wait, there is a young guy with a mike enthusing at huge volume about a new flavour of *Sabritas* crisps (they're the Mexican *Walkers* with marketing that makes Gary Linneker look well…grey) - extra chilli and lime; not surprising really. I have a quick scan to see if there are any freebies. I suspect there is a catch like taking over the mike spot for ten minutes.

Anyway, his target market is obviously younger - meaning no one over twenty-two is likely to get any free samples.

The guy is there for three hours and is tremendously successful, judging by the number of empty packets in our front courtyard by lunchtime. They fill a large refuse bag.

Does this count as a tick for everyday life or genuine culture? I am beginning to get fed up with the guide books. Nothing seems to fit.

It is time to call in another man who can provide a solution. We need big gates, in a hurry. Now this does sound unfriendly - like pulling up the drawbridge - but the truth is that almost all houses in Mérida, especially the ones in Centro, are very private with nothing visible from the street unless the occupants leave their door open at night to get the breeze.

Cue Señor K. Yes he can put us in touch with a carpenter and he is around without delay. Martin has already made a computer image of what we want. No problem. His price is very reasonable. Especially compared with an alternative quote we get from a smart outfit off the Paseo Montejo who promise to make us 'exquisite bespoke gates' for a price that would raise eyebrows in the UK.

'Mahogany or cedar?'

Oh dear. It is like a big finger is pointing at us out of the sky: 'Yes you are the destroyers of the rain forest'.

The problem is that soft wood rots very quickly in the tropics if the termites don't get there first. So hardwood is the only realistic option for anything that is going to be outside.

We go for cedar in the hope it is more eco-friendly than mahogany.

Two weeks later, the gates are installed, looking just like Martin's picture.

Peace at last. The traffic noise is muffled and the students have to throw their litter somewhere else - apart from the enterprising ones who post it in our letter box. No more loud laughs from the pavement, which always seem to coincide with some domestic mishap like dropping the tortillas into a bucket of floor cleaner. And no more wondering if we are really supposed to be joining in that earnest conversation that is going on for hours late at night just outside the gate.

So now all we have to do is get some furniture for the apartments, create a tasteful and relaxing environment and we will be motoring. It'll be easy, won't it?

Chapter 7: The great rocking chair hunt

There is a secret to shopping in Mérida. If you see something you need, you must buy it there and then. If you go away and think about it, ten times out of ten, it will have gone when you go back later having finally decided that you really do want it.

Helpfully, quite often shops selling the same thing are all in the same area - one road just south of the central square is always very fragrant as it is lined with florists. Another street is a riot of colours from all the piñatas hanging outside the stalls. These are the papier mâché and crêpe paper covered hollow figures that are very popular at parties. A load of sweets is inserted into the figure, and then party guests are blindfolded and given a stick to bash the piñata. They continue this until it breaks open and the goodies shower down. The shops have shelf after shelf of bags of sweets, just for this purpose.

On a quest for a *Sponge Bob Square Pants* piñata with a visiting young nephew, I also pick up a three foot fish with googly eyes - apparently the schoolmaster from *Finding Nemo*. There is no way I am going to bash it to pieces, and it ends up in the condo in Akumal.

Does a cartoon piñata count as genuine culture? I say it does.

However, later it is rumoured that one set of guests at Akumal have stormed out of a unit there because they can't take another moment of the decorations. Our manager Roberto diplomatically keeps stumm about which one. If it is ours, I imagine it is the plate on the wall by the dining table, showing a Mayan human sacrifice, that does it - not a cartoon fish.

At Christmas the piñata stalls sell large stars with paper streamers hanging from each point, Santas, reindeer and Christmas trees. But the staples are all the characters from recent cartoon films - our nephew eventually plumps for the lion from *Madagascar* - leaving his parents really worried they will have to pay for another seat on the plane home, as there is no way he is going to fit into an overhead locker (the piñata that is).

Shopping is fine if you can find the right street otherwise you can get really stuck.

The expats' blog on the Mérida Insider website is full of cries for help from newcomers. The hot topic is vacuum cleaner bags. I suspect these pleas are from people who haven't yet clicked that a vacuum spews out a cloud of hot air, which knocks you sideways in this heat. You might as well have left it back home, let alone worrying about replacement bags.

So it's back to basics with brooms and mops. Though to be honest, we seem to be the only people too mean to employ a maid to do this for us. The 'maid' often turns out to be a student who has to do the cleaning at 7 at night to fit in with lectures and other jobs, although wealthier households still have someone who lives in or comes in every day.

Two young Mayan women from a village outside Mérida knocked on our door back in November, just after we bought the house, asking if we needed domestic help. Well actually I had no idea what they were asking for, as I couldn't understand a word they were saying.

Then one of the workmen appeared. He had a chat with them. They were talking in Mayan. He did a simultaneous translation into Spanish. I understood a few words, feeling rather ashamed. They wanted live-in work as maids.

We felt really mean when we had to say no. The double language barrier might be problematic; also we were hoping we could start off by doing all the work ourselves. Yes, we had amateur written all over us.

Oh, if only there was an *Ikea* here. It would make life so much easier - but after all, we came here because it is different.

First, we have to find curtains. There is a curtain, blind and flooring shop just around the corner. It has a green carpet, like artificial grass, leading up to the front door to entice people in.

Armed with measurements and some Spanish phrases tortuously

prepared in advance, we head around one afternoon. We are greeted by a young assistant, who after a few faltering words in Spanish from us, responds with perfect English. More shame, embarrassment - and relief. After we have chosen some very nice fabric, said yes please we would like eight cushions to match, and he has done the sums, the final quote is astronomical - comparable with the kind of prices charged by an expensive shop in the UK. We thank him and retreat to have a think.

'I saw a great mini sewing machine in *Walmart* for 20 dollars - maybe we could make them instead?'

Martin looks dubious.

'Have you ever done pleats?'

'No!'

'Right then.'

Next try is the supermarket to see if they have any ready-made curtains. Only a few, mainly the net curtain type and not the right size anyway.

Never mind, there are several fabric shops downtown - maybe they will make up curtains? We head down to bustling Centro. People still make their own clothes here. Plus there are events like Carnaval that need new costumes every year. So there are shops packed with fabrics of all types - from cheap and cheerful cottons to expensive silks for wedding dresses.

At Christmas, they come out with a whole range of seasonal fabrics covered with Santas, nativity scenes, even snowmen, so that everyone can make new table cloths, children's clothes and other articles for Navidad.

There is quite an art, though, in buying fabric.

First you need to find a floor-walker to price up the material you want and cut it for you. (There are signs up warning against trying to bribe them to give you extra material that is not declared). They give you a chit, which you take to the cashiers.

The cashier takes your money and stamps the chit.

Finally, you head for the collection desk where your material is waiting, ready-wrapped for you. As I learn the hard way, it always pays to observe first to get the hang of the system, otherwise you may end up looking a complete idiot trying to pay at the wrong desk for about half an hour before the penny drops.

I say this is worth a tick for everyday life.

And we have a nice surprise: if you buy the material, they will make up the curtains for free.

'There's got to be a catch.' declares Martin. 'There always is. I bet it's only for the really expensive material.'

Not true; you can have whichever fabric takes your fancy.

So we chose our material - to hell with restrained prints - we go for a pure Mexican design in primary colours of red, blue and green with giant yellow sun flowers all over.

Vivid colours - big tick. Good taste - meaning neutral colours - cheerio and good riddance.

You put a 50% payment down and pay the rest on collection a week later. We can even afford to splash out on some matching cushions.

Next, we need some rocking chairs. We have got it into our heads that these are must-haves to create the right impression, after studying a book of photos of the old haciendas. They all have wonderful colonnaded courtyards with groups of rocking chairs arranged in the shade.

Strangely, no one ever seems to be sitting in them in the pictures - like no one ever seems to sit in the rocking chairs on every porch in the houses just beyond Centro, that have front gardens instead of being straight onto the pavement. It looks like these chairs are treated as family heirlooms. Maybe no one is *allowed* to sit in them. They come in all styles from old wooden chairs, carefully polished, to modern white-painted metal ones. We even spot angular art deco rocking chairs that have been coloured pale fuchsia and cream to match the house.

Now Lucia's furniture is still sitting very comfortably in our living room. We've already managed to persuade her to sell us her massive old chest of drawers and matching mirror with big swirling carvings on the front that we have fallen in love with. But no way will she sell us the fantastic over-size rocking chair in incredibly chunky wood. And she comes to fetch it back soon afterwards, to stop it feeling too at home in our house.

So it looks like finding second-hand rocking chairs might be quite difficult. Or impossible. Then again, maybe we just don't know where to look.

Early on, Dan and Sofi pointed us in the direction of a second-hand furniture shop on Calle 62, quite close to our house. They bought a table there for their fax machine but they have had most of their furniture hand-made and are planning a trip to Oaxaca for extra items because they can't find what they want in Mérida. We know they have very high standards.

The shop on Calle 62 is a great jumble of furniture cast-offs: old wardrobes with crazed mirror doors, dusty chandeliers a few drops short, rattan garden sets of sofas and tables that have seen many tropical downpours - and even rocking chairs. And it is here that we earlier bought a set of eight rustic pine dining chairs - probably cast-offs from a restaurant - for about 120 dollars the set. But though they have a fast turnover of stock, the rocking chairs are somehow never the right ones. Either the seats need re-caning or the backs are too low.

One day, I am quite taken with a deco set of four rocking chairs with a table and one ordinary chair thrown in for 100 dollars. They may have been painted a kind of dog-poo brown, but we could repaint them vibrant Cobált blue - a very popular colour here. Martin puts his foot down. He has set his heart on the high-backed elegant old wooden chairs in our hacienda book. Nothing else will create the right image. He's already pictured them under the archway - our substitute for a colonnaded terrace.

We scour the phone book that *Telmex* generously gave us when we took out our contract so that we could tantalise ourselves with all the numbers we couldn't phone. There is a colour advertisement for a firm that supplies furniture to hotels but somehow it looks expensive, plus its showroom is on the outskirts of town.

Sometime before, we took a bus to the north of town, up Calle 60, a road that stretches for miles, and along the way passed a patch of grass where someone had set up a display of newly-made fairly high quality furniture. At that point, we had been looking for carved bed heads, thinking they would add a nice touch. We got off the bus confidently expecting good prices as it was 'direct to the public'. In fact they were quite expensive so we gave up on that idea. And they didn't have any rocking chairs anyway.

We try the blog on *Mérida Insider*. Other people have asked the same question: where do you go to buy furniture? Well, one blogger points out that there are plenty of a-bit-of-everything shops in Centro that sell fridges, cookers, dining and sofa sets and washing machines. We have found a rustic table at a very reasonable price in one of these shops, to match the chairs we had already acquired second-hand. But they don't seem to have any rocking chairs.

Someone else suggests a road off the Prolongación Montejo, the northern extension of the Paseo - they haven't *actually* been there themselves although rumour has it there are several furniture shops. One of the charms and exasperations of living in Mérida is that many things are never quite definite somehow. Still, it's a strong lead and well worth following up.

One afternoon on a not too hot day (meaning it is in the mid eighties, not nineties), we decide to get some exercise and take a walk to investigate. We set off confidently up the Paseo Montejo, past the anthropological museum in one of the grand old mansions (the architectural equivalent of a wedding cake with all its stucco decorations), past the Monumento a la Patria in the middle of the roundabout at the top of the Paseo.

This is the Mérida version of Mount Rushmore with massive carvings depicting the city's Mayan ancestors, their struggles and heritage. It's sixties brutalist in design. And love it or loathe it, you can't ignore it especially when the tour buses go round and round to make sure you see it all.

North of the monument, the Paseo becomes the Prolongación and turns into a massive car showroom with dealerships for BMW, Mercedes, Chrysler, Audi and even Jaguar lining the road.

'I like that,' says Martin, reading a sign. They don't call them 'second-hand cars' here. 'Semi-nuevo' - half-new. That's even better than 'pre-owned.'

We've heard there are pitfalls in buying a second-hand car. The seller must give you the original tax and other documentation for every year since its manufacture. Someone we meet has to go to court to get their vehicle regularised as some of the papers the seller handed over turned out to be photocopies, not originals. This is still going on two years after they bought the car and will probably end up costing more than the vehicle in the first place.

After passing all the gleaming cars (they must wash them several times a day with all the dust in this city), we suddenly find ourselves in an American suburb. Neon signs advertise massive branches of *McDonalds*, *Pizza Hut*, *TGI Friday's*, *Burger King* - you name it. There are also smaller Italian and Chinese restaurants with tables set up on every available inch of outside space.

This is where people come to eat, especially at weekends. I guess you can get tired of tortillas sometimes. The richer kids here - especially the ones who get ferried around in 4-by-4s, like anywhere in the world - are getting fat and there are campaigns to persuade people to eat more tortillas, refried beans and traditional food instead of burgers and fries. In contrast, poor children in rural areas in the Yucatán have to have special school dinners because they are malnourished.

All the same, Martin stops to look at the colour pictures of triple cheese deckers on a sign.

'Maybe we could stop for a burger?'

'But just think how much more we could get for our money at one of the little places near home.'

'They're all closed in the evenings.'

'Perhaps we can call in on the way back.'

Now I know why it's so difficult for parents to say no to their children when they've been hooked by the burger chain marketing ploys. If we go there, we'll lose all our ticks for Real Mexican Food.

Past the eateries, there are wide residential roads with long low modernist houses, all angles and glass, in big gardens. This must have been *the* place to live in the fifties and sixties. It is obviously still a place to live if you have made some money. After the bustle of Centro, it all seems eerily quiet and surreal like an empty set for *Desperate Housewives*. Sprinklers are playing on large manicured lawns, the blinds firmly drawn on the huge ceiling to floor windows. Balconies are empty - not a rocking chair in sight. Well maybe they have sold them to the furniture shops just round the corner.

Martin stops and checks the map.

'This really doesn't look like an area that will have junk shops.'

And he is right. Somehow our idea of furniture doesn't seem to be quite the same as other people's. They are obviously after top notch pieces - money no object - that will not embarrass them when *Architectural Digest* comes to do the article about their home.

There is no row of shops stacked full of semi-nuevo rocking chairs as somehow we have been imagining. A small shop - correction, salon - displays some exquisitely hand painted pieces that would not have looked out of place at Versailles in its heyday. Further along, very modern blinds, furniture and objects in bright colours are on display in an architect-designed showroom like a goldfish bowl. It almost looks like *Ikea* - except it is obvious that the prices are going to be something else.

'Maybe they'll be further along.'

We keep on walking to the next junction and that is it! After trudging several miles, we decide to turn around and look for a bus, but we end up walking all the way home again with sore feet, just to spite ourselves for our foolish optimism. And we are so fed up, we forget all about the burgers.

Next morning, though, we are back on the trail. I remember an antique shop off Calle 60 close to the centre I once wandered around and left quickly after finding out the prices. You never know - they might have some rocking chairs.

The shop rambles through the ground floor of a grand old house - one room furnished with bedroom furniture, another as a formal salon. An interior courtyard is chock full of things for the garden - wrought iron seats, statues, fancy brass plant pots. Birdsong drifts down from inside the glass cupola that covers the courtyard.

This time when I go in, the rooms are more than half empty. It looks like the place is closing down. Well maybe they will have a few nice rocking chairs going cheap? Dream on. When I ask the guy at the desk, he says he knows someone who might have some rocking chairs in her bodega. He writes me a cryptic note:

'Cecilia Germon a lado de la casa del Lagarto Calle 61 x 62 y 64.'

This looks more promising. Martin is getting fed up walking all over Mérida but I persuade him it is almost a dead cert we will find the rocking chairs of our dreams. If we don't try, we will never know.

So that afternoon we are off again. Calle 61 is south of the main square, a fairly drab street with mundane shoe and mobile phone shops although a new gold emporium aimed at tourists is being fitted out on the corner closest to the centre.

Right in the middle of the street is a really astonishing house. It curves back from the busy road in a perfect half circle around a tree-filled front courtyard. A balcony runs all the way around at first floor level. The beautifully decorated stucco façade hasn't seen much paint recently. It is like something out of García Márquez, existing in a more magical parallel world. And to add to the atmosphere when we arrive classical music is being played at high volume somewhere in the interior.

Definitely worth several ticks for vibrant architecture.

We peer through the locked wrought-iron gates that separate it firmly from the hoi polloi outside. Oh wow, stacked away under the colonnade are just the kinds of rocking chairs we are after. A plaque on the wall confirms that it is *La Casa del Lagarto.*

According to our note, the shop should really be next door and the only place we can see - if it is a shop - is heavily shuttered. You never know in Mérida if this means it ceased trading several years ago or the owner has just popped out for lunch.

Maybe the shop stores its special stock in the grand house? A rather well-dressed couple can be glimpsed sitting behind the empty fountain in the courtyard. I call out, feeling like the foolish person in a fairy tale who dares to get into the castle through bluster alone. The very elegant woman comes over to the gate.

I show her my note.

Ah, I will have to come back later, maybe tomorrow after 11 am - the shop is next door and it is closed. I don't dare ask her if she could sell us her old rocking chairs instead. I feel it would be vulgar.

So we drag ourselves home again feeling tantalised. We need to get some cans of refried beans so we take a different route back, past a branch of the *San Francisco* supermarket.

'I really am getting fed up with this,' complains Martin. 'None of your bright ideas has turned up anything.'

'You just have to be persistent here. I'm sure we'll find them.'

'Well yes, one day maybe. Soon: I doubt.'

We are trudging rather grumpily along when Martin suddenly stands stock still. Oh dear I think, storm approaching - he seems peculiarly agitated - but no, he reaches out and turns my head:

'Just look at that!'

And there, inside a large dusty stockroom, in a pool of light are two rocking chairs, just the kind we have searched so long for. We retrace our steps to the shop entrance. It is a branch of *Casa Juanes.* How come we haven't tried them before? Now we feel silly. Never mind, we found them eventually.

They are about 200 dollars each - steep for our budget but they are hardwood and we manage to negotiate a discount for two. However, we get cold feet at the last moment and decide we need to think about it first before spending the money.

By the morning though, Martin is really keen to go back and get them. I still hold out hopes of finding some second hand ones in Señora Germon's shop. Martin folds his arms. 'I am not going back there. It won't be open and it won't have rocking chairs'.

'Please, just one last try and then we will go to *Casa Juanes* if she doesn't have any.'

'OK but she won't have any, I promise you, if the shop is open, which it won't be'

Phew, I breathe a sigh of relief when we get down there. The shutters have been pulled up and a table piled with old books is out on the street. A huge range of interesting junk and second hand books fills the interior. We squeeze inside. Hooray, Señora Germon is here.

Does she have any rocking chairs?

She will have a look. She disappears into the jumble behind the counter.

Yes.

Hooray.

But only children's ones.

Oh well.

We thank her and squeeze out again.

'Now', says Martin, 'we are going to *Casa Juanes.* And then we are going home. I have really had enough of furniture shops for a long time.'

Chapter 8: It's Mex Mex, not Tex Mex

With the rocking chairs finally in place, we feel we are making progress at last. Towards what exactly is another matter. Somehow, we seem to be dragging our feet about actually opening the B & B. Martin is designing a website, but we still need to get beds and fridges for the apartments. Our idea is that we will offer breakfast for shorter stays. The ideal solution will be guests who take an apartment for longer, say a month, and are happy to self-cater. Perhaps this is being over optimistic?

So I need to turn my mind to a thorny question:

What do you offer for breakfast in the tropics? Or more likely, what do guests expect? And will they walk out if they don't get exactly what they want?

Our own breakfasts do not involve much work. Fruit jelly (childish but it gives you liquid), then 'bigotes' meaning moustaches. These are chocolate filled pastry rolls in packets from the supermarket. We do make real coffee, though, after years of having no time for anything except instant. Somehow this package doesn't seem quite adequate for paying guests.

We have seen adverts in the monthly tourist magazine - *Yucatán Today* -

for a B & B downtown that always offers a long list of breakfast specials, both Mexican and American. An example for just one month is daunting:

- Huevos rancheros (fried egg on fried tortilla with chilli, onion, tomato, cream and coriander).
- Molettes (grilled toast spread with refried beans and melted cheese, topped with salsa).
- Spiced apple empanadas (pastry turnovers).
- Fruit smoothies (including mango, pineapple and papaya).
- Fresh-baked banana muffins.
- Hotcakes with honey and chocolate sauce.
- 'Plus all our regular breakfast items'.

This is some list. Secretly I am thinking they are trying too hard - maybe there is something wrong with the rooms? Somehow, I feel that is unlikely. We are up against stiff competition.

Perhaps we should offer an all-chocolate breakfast? After all this is where chocolate came from. You can buy discs of chocolate, generally spiced with cinnamon and quite bitter to make into drinks in all the supermarkets. Why not offer this and chocolate yogurts, bigotes (crisped in the oven, hopefully no one will know they are not home-made), fruit with optional chocolate sauce and a hot savoury dish with mole?

Before we came to Mexico we'd read that Yucatecan cooking often uses mole - supposedly a chocolate sauce - and being confirmed chocoholics, were keen to try it the first time we ever visited.

The hotel receptionist back in Playa gave us directions to a restaurant some blocks away from Fifth Avenue. After the va va voom spicy potato wedges with everything of Tex Mex restaurants in the UK, the real thing can seem a let down at first: meat in sauce with a mound of rice, a pool of refried beans and some salad garnish. Or try one of the endless variations on shredded chicken or turkey in or on tortillas with a marinade. But when you taste it…

The restaurant was the real thing, with a mostly Mexican clientele, not a flaming cascade of brandy in sight.

We ordered chicken in mole. We had been hoping that the sauce was like melted chocolate - or the sweet spiced chocolate drink we tasted at *Cadbury World* in Birmingham where, standing in a crowd about half our height, we first learnt the history of our favourite food. Mole is not really sweet at all: it has a slightly musty, earthy taste, not too spicy hot yet still very rich. Made from chillies, shredded tortilla, cacao and spices including cinnamon, it is an acquired taste and we wasted no time in acquiring it.

Bottles of mole are easily picked up in the supermarket, so we don't have to make our own. Maybe we could do our own version of papadzules - hard boiled eggs with mole on top?

Then again, could we go for a unique selling point and offer full English cooked breakfast? After all, it's something everyone looks forward to when they go to a B & B back in the UK. Tomatoes, eggs, mushrooms and fried bread - no problem. Sausages and bacon? Chorizos, richly spiced local sausages will make a tasty alternative to bangers. Or salchichas - really Frankfurters - might be more digestible at breakfast.

And this is the land of cochinita pibil (clay-oven cooked suckling pig) and endless varieties of pork crackling snacks so bacon shouldn't be too hard to source. And, if we really want to copy the great British B & B breakfast, what about the square cardboard toast dreaded by anyone who doesn't want the full English back home? The supermarkets sell two foot long '*Wonder*' sliced processed loaves - ideal. Then again, maybe that will be going too far for authenticity? Perhaps we could do marmalade muffins instead?

There is an orange tree in the garden, right up against the swimming pool - we didn't want to move it when the pool was excavated in case it died but now the branches are hanging over the water. So there is a possibility guests could be brained by a falling orange while taking a dip.

Last November, when we bought the house, the oranges were ripe. We thought it would be great to go out and pick our own oranges. Well, actually they turn out to be sour oranges, very, very sour and with a high ratio of pips to flesh. They will come in useful if we ever try making 'poc chuc', which is a Yucatecan pork dish marinated in sour orange juice. Otherwise, they will probably be best for marmalade, being something like Seville oranges. Well I am saying all this very confidently when I've never made marmalade before.

'And I don't like marmalade anyway,' Martin protested, 'why can't you try chutney instead?'

As there aren't any on our tree now, I go to the market to buy some oranges, and find a recipe on the internet for orange chutney. I then spend an afternoon in the kitchen in a sauna of spiced orange steam.

Well, it goes a chutney sort of colour in the end, though I ruin the pan as I leave it boiling just too long, and a kind of sticky toffee clamps itself to the bottom.

The moment of truth comes. Martin takes a small spoonful and tastes.

'It's marmalade chutney! But alright I suppose.'

I've produced a new hybrid.

Never mind, it will be excellent for semi-sweet, semi-savoury muffins when I get my culinary confidence back to try making them.

And in the absence of *Branston* pickle, it comes out with the cheese every day, so there might be none left by the time we start the B & B anyway…

In the meantime, for inspiration, we decide to try out the breakfast buffet in what is now one of our favourite cafés - *La Flor de Santiago.*

We've learnt that this is very much where men come to escape domestic ties, drink coffee and chat, and women are only really welcome with a male partner or in sedate groups for breakfast.

One wall is covered by huge blown-up copies of two colourful and busy paintings of fairs and fiestas in Mérida's main square. To the side, there is a long counter with bakery items for sale. A steady stream of people come in and buy the fresh bread, cake in large slabs similar to Madeira, and polvorone biscuits (almond shortbread rounds) all infused with a smoky taste from the wood-fired oven.

At 45 pesos a head, the café's all-you-can-eat buffet at weekends is fantastic value and means you can skip lunch. And whereas in the evening, it is pleasantly uncrowded and leisurely, at breakfast it is buzzing with almost all tables full.

To start, there are large trays of sliced fruit - no doubt from the market jut across the road. Half a dozen or more hot dishes are being constantly replenished by waiters. What did we say about Tex Mex? Hold on, here are potato skins filled with cheese and bacon, going just as fast as the hotcakes in the next dish along. Mini omelettes, molettes, empanadas filled with mince meat, and - of course - refried beans are also on offer.

If these don't take your fancy, there are plastic beakers filled with variously coloured blancmange type milk puddings.

Martin tries the pale yellow banana one, makes some faces, and says it is 'quite interesting'. Milk pudding is very popular here. If you can't get any other dessert, there will always be 'flan' on offer. This is not, as you might hope, a tropical fruit tart, but a version of crème caramel. Not the most exciting of puddings if you have a hankering for chocolate fudge cake and banoffee pie.

I prefer the freshly baked cake with raisins - made with evaporated milk to give an extra rich texture. This is all washed down with plenty of coffee or liquados - chilled milk or water with fruit juice and sugar - lemon, melon or jamaica (hibiscus, which is the closest thing you can get to *Ribena* blackcurrant drink in colour, if not taste, and very refreshing).

We can't match that breakfast. Then again, we could always point people down to Santiago at the weekends. And we will keep it simple at home, being very careful not to offer freshly squeezed orange juice. This sounds terrible but we've calculated that one small glass will need about six oranges - the cost is not the issue - it is the volume of orange skins generated that might cause problems with the refuse storage and disposal.

Cartons it will have to be, or one of the syrups - jamaica, tamarind or apple - available from the supermarket. You can also get a concentrate of horchata - rice water flavoured with cinnamon, to dilute with water.

So breakfast is kind of sorted. We also need to recommend places for evening meals, which means we will just have to go and try them all ourselves first. Great, but we also have a budget to stick to, as we have no income for the coming summer months. So we will have to avoid the flashier restaurants aimed at tourists - with tourist prices - in Centro. These are all written up in the guide books anyway. Plus, as the books point out, in Mérida price is frequently not a good indication of quality or value.

We are keen to track down the kind of places where we can get a meal for two at 100 pesos (about 10 dollars) or less, including drinks. This is certainly not hard at lunchtimes. As we've already discovered, all the markets have rows of loncherias where you can buy a filling snack for around 30 or 40 pesos - that is if you don't feel queasy watching the stall holders tear strips of turkey off a carcass with their bare hands and then add slices of avocado, tomato and lettuce, carefully fingered into position on top of a deep fried tortilla. Better to stick to hot sopa de lima in those places if you're not a local with the right friendly bacteria already in residence.

Or try one of the cocinas económicas that seem to operate out of several front rooms in every street. A blackboard outside usually has two or three dishes for that day to eat in or take away. By eleven on weekday mornings, enticing cooking smells waft out over the hot pavements.

One lunchtime, returning from Santa Ana market I decide to pick up some lunch on the way, as we have fallen into a cheese, bread and tomato rut, which is cheap but monotonous.

Two ladies in their fifties are running a new cocina out of the crumbling corner room of an old colonial house. They have a trestle table set up with an assortment of plastic and metal containers. Behind them a couple of huge vats are bubbling away.

I order the 'Tortillas de papa' imagining something like a Spanish omelette. Somehow I don't think I quite manage to get with the programme as I end up with two multi-sectioned polystyrene containers filled with:

- Spicy deep fried potato cakes made with - nothing except potato.
- Generous portions of spaghetti in home-made tomato sauce.
- Shredded lettuce and tomato.

- And vinegary pickles to round the meal off.

All hand picked out of the various containers.

'Where's the protein?' Martin demands when I get back.

'I think I was supposed to ask for it.' I say.

'Better get the cheese out again.' says Martin, sounding resigned.

'But it only cost 50 pesos altogether.'

'Just as well.'

And it is very tasty, Martin has to agree.

However, something even better is just a few blocks up Reforma. All over the Yucatán there are smoke houses where pieces of chicken are cooked on a bed of charcoal. There is one in the next road that always seems to have a queue at weekend lunch times.

People will disappear into the dark smoke-filled interior and emerge triumphantly with a big plastic bag filled with smoked chicken, rice, pickles and corn tortillas. The one time we venture in must be a slow day and there is a cloud of hungry flies circling the charcoal grill. We leave quickly, empty handed.

Further up the road is a superior establishment, despite its silly name - *Chicken Itzá*. Here the chicken is speared on a rotisserie and you can be sure it is freshly cooked. You place your order - a quarter, half or whole -and the chicken will be carried in tongs to a tray and then cut up with enormous scissors.

With the chicken come medium pickles and hot pickles and a bag of warm tortillas. Also on offer as a side dish is ensalada de mayonesa (basically what is known in the catering trade as Russian salad - potato cubes with peas and diced carrots in mayonnaise). This is collected from the fridge out the back and always comes with ten *Ritz* biscuits. Tastier is the spicy saffron rice with shredded chicken in it. After a few visits, we drop the chicken and just order half a kilo of rice and half a kilo of spaghetti in tomato sauce - for under four dollars. This lasts several meals and is probably as cheap as making it ourselves.

One dish we do often make for ourselves is quesadillas, which is the Mexican equivalent of toasted cheese and very filling.

Take a medium sized flour tortilla, spread it with salsa or tomato ketchup if pushed, layer on thinly sliced manchego cheese and top with canned sliced mushrooms (much easier and cheaper to get then fresh mushrooms in the Yucatán). Then fold the tortilla over on itself into a half moon and shallow fry (this gives a nice crispy outside - dry frying, which is the more traditional way, leaves the tortilla floppy) in hot oil for about twenty seconds on each side.

Serve with guacamole, salsa, refried beans and rice. Manchego cheese melts very easily - and has a better taste than Dutch semi-hard cheeses which are about the closest you can get to it back home. In the UK, it's best to use grated cheddar as it melts well and has more flavour.

A superior version of quesadillas is syncronizadas - take one flour tortilla and top with a layer of manchego cheese, then a layer of smoked ham, then another layer of cheese. Place another tortilla on top so its edges match up with the one below and cook the same way as quesadillas. When cooked, cover with sautéed mushrooms with a dollop of sour cream on top.

Either version only takes a few minutes to prepare. We might even offer them for breakfast.

If guests get really desperate for a quick snack in the evening, they can always pop over to the food stands outside the university that do a busy trade with the students attending evening lectures. Here you can take your pick from:

- Chips with a garnish of pieces of salchicha cut open to look like flowers, and a slice of lime.
- Pancakes cooked to order in a griddle with a lid that clamps down on the batter.
- Corn on the cob cored so that you can squirt in a sauce and eat the whole thing.

The café next door also does a roaring trade in snacks up to nine thirty at night. Their chicken is said to be very, very good. The problem is, we are still embarrassed over the refuse issue and have yet to muster enough courage to go in there.

If you get tired of Mexican, there is always pizza. Our favourite place that comes in under budget is *Vito Corleone's* down in Centro. The only problem is that it is shoehorned into a tiny space with a balconied seating area just above the pizza oven. So it is an incredibly sweaty place to be at any time in a tropical climate, despite the turbo fans. The pizza is great though - very thin dough that you eat with your hands as no cutlery is provided. Plus - in case you are feeling the cold - there is a hot, hot Mexican version piled with chorizo and chillies.

And what about that mysterious pink café, *Restaurant Reforma*, just a minute's walk away? One day we decide to have another try. We'd been spooked the first time so we felt like the silly kids in a horror film who go back to the bad old house even though everyone is telling them: you don't want to do that.

Tonight, there is someone there. A very sedate older lady with a big pan on the table in front of her is sitting right under the TV. She has a pile of plantain leaves to her side and is busy making something.

We hesitate and then, magically, an old guy appears from nowhere with some plastic covered menus and ushers us to a table. He takes our drinks order and disappears into the depths of the house. The busy lady smiles at us. We are the only people here.

A loudspeaker in the corner crackles and then starts playing Chopin in heavy competition with the TV that is showing *Los Sánchez*, a popular and rambunctious sitcom. We recognise Tito, one of the central characters with long floppy hair and the kind of highlights that stop you dead in your tracks. This is going to be an interesting evening.

A motherly lady emerges from the distant kitchen and recites the specials at high speed. She is really encouraging us to go for flautas - we haven't a clue what they are, but decide to pick them anyway.

I indicate to the lady by the TV and ask: 'Tamales?' She says they won't be ready until tomorrow. They are very fiddly to make and incredibly filling. Rather like a giant savoury *Nutri-Grain* bar, a core of marinated meat is covered in a coat of corn meal mixed with lard then wrapped up in the plantain leaves and steam cooked.

So tonight we are going to have flautas, whatever they are. To keep us going while we wait, the waiter brings us each a free botana - a spicy empanada, like a mini cornish pasty - plus salsa and tortilla chips - much better than you get in many more expensive restaurants. In fact, in the more pretentious restaurants, tortilla chips seem to be considered down market although you will be lucky to get bread instead.

No sooner have we finished our empanadas but the flautas arrive. Ah, flutes - a whole row of them. Spicy chicken and pickled red onion has been tightly wrapped in corn tortillas and then deep fried until crunchy. The flutes are laid in a row on the plate and covered with sour cream, sprinkled with powdered cheese and topped with shredded lettuce. It all adds up to quite a plateful that is extremely tasty.

This has suddenly become our favourite restaurant. And the mystery is solved by a closer study of the menu - its main business is home delivery and special parties in the restaurant itself. There has only ever been one other table occupied - and only on one occasion - all the times we have been there. But we always get our own ambient music.

Real Mexican food - big, big tick.

Chapter 9: Hi, it's me, Emily

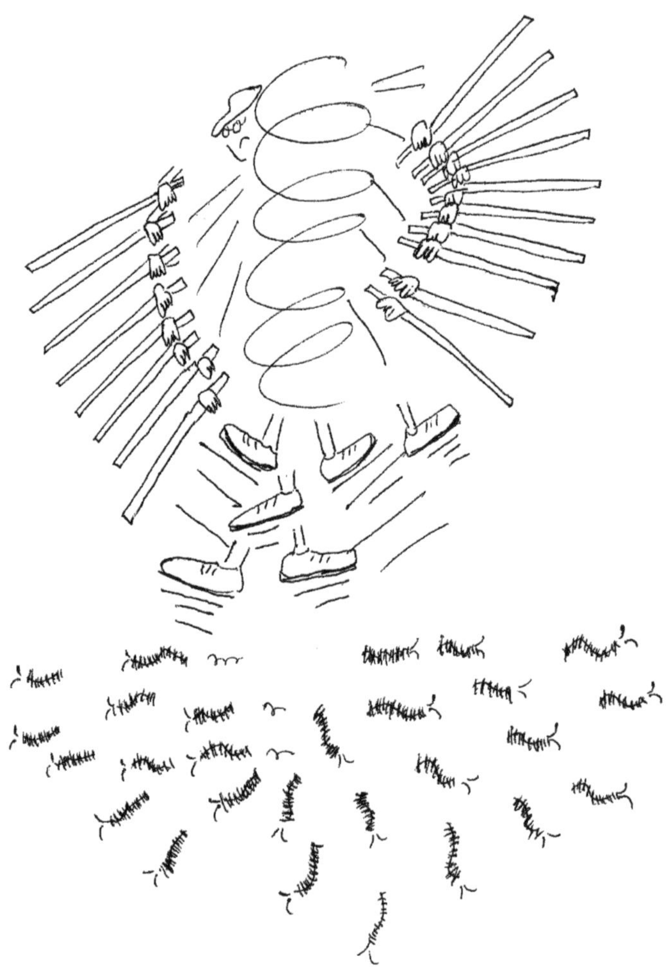

June and the rainy season has started.

By the end of the month, we've got a wardrobe full of every type of cheap rain cape you can buy, from the plastic-bag-with-holes-for-arms-and-head to the fancy yellow one with metal button and pocket detail.

We walk off somewhere in dazzling sunshine, the sky's a clear blue and then suddenly it clouds over towards late afternoon, a wind from nowhere starts gusting viciously, a couple of big blobs of rain hit your face then pow.

The streets turn into rivers - you suddenly realise why the pavements are two feet off the ground - and you wade through water up to the ankles to cross the road. Rain hammering on the corrugated roofs of the big supermarkets drowns out the Muzak - and sales of brollies and macs soar as taxis disappear as fast as endangered species.

At least the rain drowns some of the mozzies, ha, ha. Then just as we are celebrating, another menace turns up. This one has hundreds and hundreds of tiny feet. Yes, it is millipede season. Martin disappears into the garden just as the sun is getting really hot after breakfast and there's the sound of cursing and stamping and thwacking with sticks for about twenty minutes. Then he comes back in with the daily toll:

'Fifty.'

'Eighty.'

'At least a hundred; I can't believe it.'

The trouble is that they hide the rest of the day under rocks and in the earth. Short of spraying the whole garden this seems the only way to keep them under control. And it does work: well about two months later the toll starts going down until there are only two or three a day. Maybe the season is over anyway.

Then just as we are relaxing, when Martin is out one day, I see something that looks like the front half of a scorpion easing itself out of a hole in the wall on the stairs, its long feelers maniacally probing the air. I grab the insecticide spray and deluge it but it keeps on advancing so I run.

A couple of hours later, I venture back to check. It is still half in and half out of the wall but looks dead. I put on some gloves and pull. About four inches of giant millipede ooze out. Yuk. I dump it in a far corner of the garden. Martin will never know. At least it isn't a scorpion. Martin checks his shoes every morning for these just in case.

Wildlife - yes. Cute - no ticks.

June is not just the start of the rainy season; it is also the official start of the hurricane season. Usually you only really expect hurricanes in September and October. That was the theory until now. Things are about to change. Not for nothing did the Mayans coin the word hurricane - meaning evil wind.

We've been taking it in turns to go back to the UK. Somebody is keeping an eye on our house back home for us but we have to leave Mexico every three months when our tourist visas expire. We haven't felt ready yet to take the leap, sell the UK house and apply for foreign residents' FM3 visas. Also we aren't sure we will get them as we need to show proof of income and at the moment we don't have any. Someday soon we have to make the big decision.

In May, I decided to resign from my job in London, after taking three months' unpaid leave. I could have taken another three if I promised to go back afterwards. We really need to give it a year. The person covering for me was fine to stay on, so I didn't feel so bad and in early June I'd gone back to say goodbye to my colleagues.

Now it is Martin's turn to go home.

He leaves early on the morning of July 7th to get a flight via Houston. I get up, go out and vacuum the pool, have breakfast and switch on the laptop to look at emails. We always check the BBC news site. Usually it is a quick glance: British politics seem remote from here. Today, I just stare at the screen in horror. There've been bombs on tube trains and a bus in London. I remember how the police kept on saying that it is not a matter of if but when there will be a terrorist attack. You still hope it won't happen.

I send an email to my former colleagues, asking if they are OK, but I know they will be too busy to reply for a while. I manage to contact my parents and they say they think everyone is safe although my brother in law, who commutes to the city, has not been in touch yet. The mobile phone systems are overloaded and it is hard for people to get through. He doesn't usually take any of the tube lines that have been hit, so he should be safe.

Martin doesn't hear the news until he gets to Houston and the immigration officer, seeing his British passport, offers his sympathies.

I go out into the bright sunshine. Back in the UK, everyone will be anxiously watching the news and discussing what has happened. Being so far away, it is really hard to take in. I know I am very, very lucky to be here in a peaceful garden in Mexico and not commuting to London.

I feel like I need to do something practical, so I get on with painting the faded walls in the front courtyard. First a trip up the road to the paint shop is needed to buy some paint to match the blue-green on the lower half of the house. I take an old paint lid with me.

The shop is a small family-run place and both father and son spend an hour trying to get the right colour for me as it is non-standard.

First comes the sound of stirring and mixing from the workshop next door, and then the noise of a hairdryer as they dry the colour, and then they appear triumphantly with a sample on a piece of cardboard. I would have been quite happy with one of the earlier results, but they have a look at it in the daylight, shake their heads and disappear back inside to do more mixing. Eventually they are satisfied and I lumber home with a large can and get going.

When we first arrived in Mérida we looked at the faded colour on a house and thought: it hasn't has a lick of paint in twenty years or more. Now we know better: it was probably done last year and no one has worked up the energy to do this year's repaint yet.

The humidity and tropical downpours wreak havoc with even the best paint job. So the only thing is to paint often and fast. We've seen teams of three workmen repaint a whole two storey mansion in under a day. The paint has to be pretty runny or it dries before you even have a chance to smooth it out with your brush.

Not to be outdone, I am determined to finish the painting by the evening and work all out for the next five hours. As it is over ninety degrees, I have to stop every ten minutes or so to take another swig of non-diet *Coke* full of lovely sugar for an energy boost. Despite this, by the time I finish at eight in the evening, I am feeling dazed and confused. After moving all the equipment back into the bodega in the garden, I lock the padlock on the archway gate behind me. Immediately I realise that:

- One: I don't have the key to the padlock on me.
- Two: The kitchen door into the garden is locked on the inside.
- Three: All the windows have bars on them.
- Four: Martin has the only other key to the house, and he is in the UK.

Therefore I am locked in the garden. And I have about ten minutes before it is totally dark.

I have to think quickly before panic sets in. I have a stepladder, great. I have the key to the front gate and door, which would be fine if I weren't stuck in the garden. The back wall is too high to get over and one side wall is the neighbouring house and even higher. I could scramble over the wall into the next garden but that's where the dogs live, fantastic. And they always sound like they are having a pitched battle so how will they react if I suddenly descend into their patch?

All is quiet at the moment. I clamber up the stepladder to do a recce. The garden is pretty overgrown. No sign or sound of the dogs. Maybe they are lurking?

I shout out a few '¡holas!', to see if the neighbours are there. I am trying to work out how to say: 'I'm stupid' in Spanish to explain my predicament. There is no response. At this rate, I am going to be stuck in the garden until Martin gets back from the UK in two weeks' time.

Sod it, I have to get out. I carefully lower the ladder down the wall. There is still no sign of the dogs. I slowly ease myself down the ladder. Nothing. I breathe a sigh of relief. Hang on; this garden has a wall all around it to keep the dogs in. And it is getting so dark I can hardly see a thing. I am sure I can hear rustlings in the undergrowth.

Gingerly, I pick up the ladder and stumble my way over to another wall that faces the road. Every moment I expect a posse of ravenous wild dogs to come flying at my ankles. Knees knocking, I manage to scramble up the ladder onto the top of the next wall. Lucky, lucky star: this must be the one day in the year the dogs actually get taken for a walk.

I'm not there yet. There is another wrought iron fence to climb over to reach the pavement.

Having avoided the dogs, I am really expecting to get arrested for trespass and suspected burglary any moment as I descend the ladder onto the pavement, trying to act casual. People are walking past but don't stop. I shoulder the ladder and trip along like this is what I do, oh most days.

Now I know how burglars get away with it. Makes you think.

On the watch for hurricanes, we have started checking the *Weather Underground* site everyday and a blog run by Jeff Masters, a well respected American meteorologist and hurricane expert. About a week after Martin gets back to the UK, I log on first thing in the morning and find Martin has sent me an urgent email:

'You'd better take a look at *Weather Underground.* Tropical Storm Emily is about to turn into a hurricane and she's heading your way'.

The trouble with hurricanes is they are only predictable up to a point. There comes a moment when a hurricane's path is pretty clear but it can gather or lose force or stall for hours. Emily is heading for the Yucatán's Caribbean coast on a course that will put Akumal directly in its path in 24 hours' time on the night of July 17th and Mérida a few hours after.

Later that morning, Roberto, the manager at Akumal, sends out an email to all ten owners:

'We are evacuating all guests inland to Cobá by the end of today. Trying to get as much furniture into the bathrooms as possible. Will stay here in the office with Morrison.'

Morrison is the resident cat and most of the time stubbornly refuses to budge from his chair in the office.

A red alert is in force on the Caribbean coast. This means that everyone has to evacuate if told to do so by the authorities unless they have good reason, and agree to sign a waiver form. Roberto, who lives in the casita on site, signs the form and carries on directing work to protect the property. Morrison has also decided evacuation is not for him.

Meantime in Mérida, the radio and TV are broadcasting amber alerts. I get used to hearing the alarm signal tune followed by public information - every car radio and shop tannoy system seems to be tuned to the same station.

All over town, people are taping up their windows. On TV, they read out the list of shelters to go to if your property is damaged in the hurricane - and show mounds of *Wonder* loaves waiting ready to feed evacuees.

Piles of palm fronds and tree branches are heaped all over the pavements as people are being urged to cut down anything that might come loose in the wind. What it will do lying all over the road is another question.

I decide that cheese spread in a jar and cereal bars will be good things to have in stock so I head along Calle 47 to the *Isstey* store on Calle 60. This is like a co-op for civil servants, although the public are allowed to shop there as well.

You can hardly move inside due to the queues of patiently waiting people with full trolleys snaking up and down every aisle. It will take hours to get out of here. So I call in at the tiny tendejon on the way home and buy *CheezWhizz* and cinnamon crackers. The previous evening, I walked up to *Walmart* as we have finally discovered this is the only place to buy bars of imported Belgian chocolate (at prices much lower than they will cost in the UK, a mere channel hop away!) I can face a hurricane as long as I have a stock of chocolate ready.

Next, I rush around the corner to the local hardware store - *Los Dos Camellos* - where we have got friendly with the owner and his wife. He refuses to speak any English with us any more, as we have had quite enough time to get going with Spanish. There is another queue. Lucia is out of town but her Mum, Marisol, who handles rentals at a real estate office over the road, is here.

'Ah Susan, are you ready?'

'I think so', I say. 'I've come to get some tape to do the windows. Er, that's about it.'

'Ah yes, but have you get a lamp? And a torch? And extra drinking water? After Isidore, that was really important.'

There is one kerosene lamp left - Marisol says I should have it but I know I will be more dangerous with it than without so I urge her to take it.

I say a big thank you to Marisol, we exchange phone numbers and good luck messages and rush off.

I think I'd better follow Marisol's advice and get another garrafon of drinking water in stock just in case.

I am thinking I could use buckets of water from the pool for washing and flushing the loo but it isn't exactly drinkable. I heave a 20 litre garrafon back from the corner shop and store it under the concrete stairs. I decide that this is going to be my hurricane shelter and have put a mattress ready. Plus a plastic bucket in case it gets too wild to venture to the loo just across the room. With a weak bladder, you must get your priorities right.

I spend the afternoon creating pretty patterns with masking tape all over the windows. Later Martin produces overwhelming evidence from the web that this is a total waste of time, and actually makes it more dangerous if the window does shatter as the pieces are bigger. Plus it's things coming in through the window that are the real problem.

It makes me feel better at the time. That is, until I remember Roberto saying that it took them days to get the tape off the windows the last time there was an alert, and in future they will just open them to give less resistance to the wind.

As up to twenty inches of rain is expected, I drain a few inches off the pool. Then I put all our valuable documents in a sandwich box and stuff it under the mattress.

I turn on the TV and see the *TreceTV* newscaster is wearing a flak jacket *in the studio.* My knees start shaking. I have to get a grip.

By the time Emily has crossed the land between the Caribbean and Mérida, she will have weakened. Isidore came the other way - Emily could never be that ferocious as hurricanes lose power when they leave the sea. It is Akumal that is in trouble. Think of Roberto and Morrison braving it out, literally in the eye of the storm.

I decide to do something positive so I put *L'Oreal* on my hair and read Agatha Christie as there's nothing like a cosy English village murder to take your mind off things. Just then, the bell rings. What a moment to get evacuated. But no, it is Sally and Jaime, who's come back over from Cancun. They are out for a walk before the curfew starts at eight, and think they will check on how I am doing. I am really pleased to see them although to be honest; all I can think of now is how ridiculous I must look with shade 4.54 plastered all over my hair.

I get out some cake and we swap tips on what to do:

'If you see your water tank flying past the window, whatever you do, don't go running after it.'

'Yes, but if you see your gas tank winging through the air, better get out quickly in case it explodes.'

'You know', says Jaime, 'often more people get killed through electrocution than anything else in a hurricane because the lines come down with the power still on.'

This is a sobering thought, especially when you have seen the spaghetti-like tangle of lines criss-crossing any road in Centro.

'I've just thought', says Sally, cheering up, and not forgetting her role as a MEL volunteer and pro-reading campaigner: 'we can catch up on all the books we've been meaning to read.'

Well maybe this is the chance I need to get to grips with *Moby Dick*. My sister picked it up when pregnant and read those opening words 'Call me Ishmael' and thought: that's a good name. I am deeply embarrassed that this is as far as I have got to date. At this rate, young Ishmael will have read it first.

We know that the hurricane won't arrive until about 10 the next morning, but when it starts to get dark they have to hurry back home, as they might be arrested for being out in what is now a red alert. They say the streets are already eerily deserted, shops closed and boarded, only emergency vehicles out on the roads and all the traffic lights taken down as a precaution, after they were smashed up by Isidore.

That night I sleep under the stairs in case Emily speeds up overnight, and get up at six. I turn on the TV and the same newscaster is still there, still in his flak jacket. He must have been on all night and the hurricane hasn't even got here yet.

I go out into the garden. No sunny blue sky this morning, just grey and overcast and the wind is really picking up. There is nothing to do except sit tight. I check the internet one more time before securing the laptop in a plastic box. Emily has made landfall over Akumal as expected - though she has dropped from a force five, which would have been catastrophic, to a force four - if that is any comfort. We have no news about how things are going over there on the coast.

The wind is increasing by the minute with all the palm trees lashing around in the garden. Forgetting about the dangers of crashing windows, I rush up stairs to get a few photos. So far, nothing that isn't supposed to be is flying around even though there are some pretty strong gusts. I hurry back down under the stairs. A couple of hours pass and then the wind starts to calm down. Phew, Mérida has been lucky - Emily has dropped right down overland to a force two, and has gone to the east where Tizimin and surrounding villages have taken some damage but nothing like as bad as feared.

Sally and Jaime are fine though disappointed that there hasn't after all been that much time for reading…

The electricity is still on so I am able to contact Martin to say all is fine, at least in Mérida. Apart that is from traffic chaos by the evening, caused by all the missing traffic lights. And in Dan and Sofi's street, they have a burst water main. The authorities temporarily turned off the city water for a few hours as a precaution and the pipes couldn't take the sudden pressure surge when it came back on again.

But what is happening in Akumal? Reports are coming in of damage - especially to Puerto Aventuras, the new marina just north of Akumal. The next morning, as torrential rain falls outside, an email comes in from the chairman of our owners' group. He's managed to speak with Roberto on his cellular phone. He and Morrison have been shaken about by the wind, but are not stirred. The eye of the hurricane passed right over Akumal, with the worst of the damage being done to the north east of the eye, as this was the strongest point of the swirling mass of wind.

Roberto actually went out in the deathly still that comes when the eye is right overhead to see how things were, making sure to get back in before the eye moved on and the ferocious wind started tearing everything up again.

Later he told us: 'It was just so strange. No sound at all except the waves. I could see all the damage but couldn't do anything and I knew there was more to come.'

They are still assessing the final damage. All the doors and windows on the first floor have been blown out. Most of the turtle nests on the beach are destroyed, and absolutely everything is wet through from the rain that followed the wind. There is no electricity or water and Roberto's phone has now packed up.

We all need to wire money as quickly as possible to fund the clear-up and repairs as it will take months for any insurance to come through. Even though there is damage in all the surrounding towns and villages, everyone turns up for work as soon as the hurricane has passed.

Meanwhile, that evening I have had enough of being housebound and go out for a walk. There is some debris on the pavements and roads and a few places blocked by fallen trees but nothing like the scene in London back in 1987 when hurricane-force winds hit the south-east of England. And the house I lived in then had really been swaying all night.

Here in Mérida, everything is pretty much as normal, just endless rain although even that is not as much as forecast. You can almost hear everyone breathing a sigh of relief all over the city.

Back in Akumal, the clear up is going at full speed but there is nowhere to stay so they don't want any of us turning up. In one apartment, the wind has pulled a fridge through two rooms and jammed it up against the front door.

There is still no electricity from Playa south to Tulum - most of the poles are down; felled as easily as a line of matchsticks - and only intermittent water. The hurricane has left a trail through the jungle that looks like a nuclear winter with every tree stripped bare of its leaves.

All the same, Roberto is confident they can get everything up and running again in a couple of weeks. What's the Mayan for 'can do'?

So that's Mexico's fair share of hurricanes for the 2005 season, isn't it? I mean, you only get a direct hit once every ten years, don't you? Wait a minute, this is only July. Jeff Masters is saying we ain't seen nothing yet. Come on guys, you can't be serious, can you?

Chapter 10: Dinosaurs are us, maybe

It is already August and, if we are serious, we need to start the final countdown to opening the B & B. OK, maybe just after a hurricane is not the best timing but we definitely have to get it together for the end of October when people will start planning their winter trips down here.

Martin has come up with a cunning plan to tempt visitors:

'Let's do customised tours for small, select groups.'

'They'll have to be very small - we haven't even got a car, let alone a minivan.'

'We'll hire one just for when we're doing the tours. I'll be tour leader and you can do the picnics and look after things when they go wrong, like someone needs to go to the toilet and we're in the middle of nowhere.'

'Fantastic, and where exactly will we be going?'

'I think we could do an end of the dinosaurs tour. You know, we're really close to the edge of the Chicxulub crater here, the one made by the meteorite that put paid to the dinosaurs sixty-five million year ago.'

'Well as long as I don't have to lie in wait in the bushes with a plastic dinosaur on my head.'

The whole geology of the Yucatán is due to this impact - creating the honeycomb effect of underground rivers and caves. Back in May, we'd gone exploring. Now I understood why Martin had been so keen to go to a place that doesn't exactly get much of a write up in the guide books - about two lines if it is lucky.

Chicxulub village, on the coast about six kilometres east of Progreso, seems to have taken the guide books seriously and does not feel like a place that appreciates its importance in history.

It's just a very small and sleepy fishing village with more dogs around than people. There are lines of concrete and wood beach houses all shuttered up, waiting for the summer crowds. A wind blows off the grey-green sea, carrying the smell of rotting seaweed from the beach.

Dramatic scenery? No ticks unless you are talking about strictly mental imagery as you close your eyes and try very hard.

'How are we going to talk this up?'

We survey the scene with sinking hearts.

Martin is undaunted:

'I've got another idea.' He unfolds a map and lays it on the beach, securing each corner with a pebble. The wind starts blowing sand all over it.

'Look.' He drops a meteorite-shaped pebble right onto Chicxulub on the map.

'You are here. Just imagine what it was like when this thing hit.'

I look around. I am finding it difficult. My imagination is refusing to stretch. I am thinking how we could put it in the tour itinerary:

'Visit to Chicxulub - epicentre of the impact. Virtually unchanged since the cataclysmic events that revolutionised the course of world history. We take time to explore and feel ourselves back into that scene of infinite devastation. (15 minutes maximum).

'This is really hard work. I think the tour will be ready for lunch quite quickly after this. What about Progreso? I wouldn't chance it here. That café place back there look like it is still recovering from the meteorite impact.'

'Lunch - Progreso (a relaxed 2 hours).'

Great idea: We can head to Progreso right now to search out a good restaurant for the tours. Now basically in Progreso food equals fish, nice and fresh, and plenty of it.

We find a restaurant - *La Viña del Mar* - overlooking the malecón, which is a broad pavement that runs along the sea front. The windows are wide open to make the most of the breeze, and this being a Sunday, practically every table is taken by family parties making a leisurely meal well into the afternoon. Sunday lunch might almost be dead in the UK; here it is still a big thing.

A waiter appears and reads out a long list of specials with evident pride. They are all fish or seafood.

'¿Tiene pollo?' He looks at us aghast. What do we want chicken for? This is madess.

To be honest, we've been put off fish that looks too much like fish forever by the regurgitated smelly flannel that we ate for primary school dinners.

Reluctantly, he accepts our order with a shake of the head and goes on to the next table, where he is ever so nice and attentive to the large family for the rest of the afternoon because they, of course, have all ordered fish.

Not that we could claim we are neglected. Once we've ordered, a whole range of free botanas magically appear: pickled octopus, sausage and potato salad, chilli prawn, gherkins and something like sauerkraut, and bread as well. It is almost a meal in itself.

When our food arrives, we think the chef has taken umbrage and given us fish anyway as it looks just like a battered filet of plaice. We don't dare say anything until the waiter has bustled on his way to the gold star table.

Martin pokes his filet tentatively.

'It's fish, I'm sure it's fish.'

I poke mine.

'Certainly feels like fish. What does it smell like?'

'The waiter's watching us. Act normal. And don't try smelling the fish whatever you do. I volunteer to have a taste.'

Martin cuts off a small corner and nibbles. He looks really shocked.

'Oh, it's chicken. Not bad actually. You can relax. The chips are good too. It's nice to have them instead of rice for a change.'

Phew, panic over.

But the chicken is sitting on the plate saying to us: Are you crazy? You come to the seaside and don't want fish?

Real Mexican Food? No, you only get ticks for fish in Progreso.

This is certainly a good place to bring a tour party - especially if they like fish. If we have a group that would rather have, say, bangers and mash then we will need a rethink.

Plus we will just have to be careful to avoid the days when the cruise boats dock at the pier and disgorge something like three thousand people in one go, all heading straight for the restaurants. We will still be queuing at midnight.

Progreso is also a good place to have a swim to freshen up before going on to the next site. The only problem is you end up swimming in about two feet of water as the sea is shallow for a long, long way out. We see people wading off towards the far horizon in the vain hope of getting to deeper water.

The beach is sandy - the only drawback being that you will not get much rest and relaxation because a different beach vendor will approach on average every two minutes.

Well, if you are in the mood for shopping, this could be a great selling point. We visualise the tour itinerary:

'Following lunch, opportunity to buy all your holiday presents (twenty minutes will be ample).'

Because in the space of a few minutes, you can choose from:

- Brightly painted wooden turtles and armadillos with wobbly heads dangling from a line of cotton fixed into the back.
- A selection of Mexican sweets - several variations on coconut ice, peanut brittle, guava paste, pastry cones with vanilla filling…
- Silver jewellery plus plenty of flattery.
- Leather belts with studwork patterns - very cowboy.
- Hammocks - you have been warned!
- Tie-die beach dresses and shorts, with labels saying 'Made in Thailand'.
- Helium cartoon character balloons - all the *Los Increíbles* family today plus a Bart Simpson if you must!

- More hammocks - including chair hammocks with a wooden rod for hanging. The kind of thing that looks a really good idea until you get home and wonder how and where the hell you are actually going to hang it.

- Squeaky toys on wheels with a pull-along pole - sausage dogs and ducks a favourite.

- Baseball caps, sunhats, umbrellas to use as parasols and also handy if it rains this afternoon, as it probably will.

- Yet more hammocks.

Some good stuff, some rubbish, some things you see on any tourist beach…

No pressure; if you want to pass over this great opportunity then no sweat amigo, have a nice day. Ah ha, I think you are interested…

Martin looks pensive after lunch. It obviously isn't the food as it has really been very tasty after all that, and extremely reasonably priced.

'I don't know, I'm beginning to think there isn't a huge amount of mileage in the Chicxulub crater. There's not exactly any smoking debris to see.'

'Could we combine it with something else? We're always saying that people are missing a treat with some of the smaller Mayan sites. Plus they're much less crowded.'

'How about the Grand Catastrophe tour? That will get people interested. We can combine Chicxulub with visiting Mayan sites and looking at their prophesy that the world will end in 2012. We can go into their astronomy and mathematics.'

'Well I guess no-one will be disappointed if the tour turns into a disaster. We can always say: What did you expect? Not like that one we went on in Jordan called 'Happy Nomads'. Now that was really tempting fate. Remember the mutiny on the coach?'

Martin is really getting into the idea:

'It'll broaden our market: we'll attract all the people who read *The Crystal Skulls* and *The Mayan Prophesies* and the other books. All those alternative theories.'

'We don't want too many crackpots on the tour.'

'Well we've read all the books and we're not crazy, are we?'

So the next stops on our scouting expedition are a few of the lesser known Mayan sites around Mérida. We assume that everyone will already have been to Uxmal and admired the House of the Turtles, the nunnery quadrangle and the Pyramid of the Magician - and probably got stuck at the top. On a previous visit, this is exactly what happened to me. I was fine getting up there. Then I looked over the side - and it was almost a totally sheer drop.

'Martin, I have a problem. How much does it cost to charter a helicopter? I don't think I can get down any other way.'

'Ner.' And I saw him hop over the edge and practically skip down.

I had to do something before I was totally paralysed with fear. Fortunately there was a chain to one side of the steps - and a steady stream of people making use of it, laboriously easing themselves down step by step while clinging for dear life to the rusty chain.

About half an hour later, I arrived back on firm ground.

'Never again.'

The authorities must have heard me because on the next visit we find that you aren't allowed to climb that pyramid anymore.

If you are lucky and get there early, you can have the site at Uxmal almost to yourself; the son et lumière is more atmospheric than the one at Chichén Itzá (where you share the experience with what feels like a football crowd). The friezes are much higher quality, though beautiful is not exactly the word for creatures - gaping serpents' mouths, grotesque semi-human faces with noses like elephants' trunks, and strange plumed gods - that make gargoyles look quite cute and friendly.

There is also the little matter of human sacrifices, which is hard to square with the peacefulness of the nunnery quadrangle at Uxmal where you can sit and watch the scaly iguanas playing hide and seek as groups of tourists drift in and out again.

That is, until you see the long lines of skulls and crossbones carved on some of the low walls. These represent just a few of the victims sacrificed to the gods so that the sun will still shine, the rain fall and the crops grow - and the ruler will look good. Some things never change.

Martin has read a book that claims it was a great honour to be chosen as a Mayan human sacrifice.

'You had a really good time for the last year of your life: living like royalty, great food, no work.'

'You haven't convinced me. I still don't think it would compensate for what happened when the sacrificial victims' year-off was over.'

'Well, they probably drugged them anyway, so they wouldn't try anything when they were being led up to the top of the pyramid.'

'I'm sure I would have had a last minute change of mind, seeing the blood stains of the last victims all over the steps. And imagine the smell.'

'You would have been thinking of what an honour it was for you and your family. And it is a quick way to go, having your heart cut out.'

'Well I can't help remembering all those situations at work where they ask for volunteers, the way the worst jobs get talked-up into a fantastic opportunity…'

We head for Dzibilchaltún, which like Chichén Itzá, has a phenomenon at the Spring and Autumn equinox. In Chichén Itzá, the play of light and shadow at sunset on one of the stepped edges of the EL Castillo pyramid looks like the feared and worshipped serpent god Kukulkan snaking his way up the side in Spring and down in Autumn.

Fantastic, but you will be joining a huge crowd of other people to witness the phenomenon. No doubt it was the same in ancient Mayan times so I suppose that makes it really authentic. And just like the modern-day druids celebrating the summer solstice at Stonehenge in the UK, white-robed Mayans perform religious ceremonies alongside the tourists.

At Dzibilchaltún there is a small pyramid known as the Temple of the Seven Dolls; because seven doll-like artefacts were found during an excavation there. Paved roads called Sacbes used to connect the important parts of Mayan cities and also one city with another. Sacbe means "white way" in Mayan. These roads were raised up above the surrounding landscape, and coated in brilliant white limestone stucco, so that they could be followed at night; the only time when it was cool enough to travel.

From the square of ancient buildings at Dzibilchaltún, you walk about a third of a mile out of the main site along a well preserved Sacbe to the Temple of the Seven Dolls, which is topped with a little room with doorways to each point of the compass. The sunrise on the equinoxes shines straight through two of these doors, so it looks like a great golden ball is being born from within the temple.

As long as it isn't misty, that is, which at sunrise is always a risk. In spring, this was the signal to the Mayans to start planting their crops. It's not clear what they did if it was overcast and the sun refused to perform.

Then again, they didn't really need signs to tell them when to do things as the Mayans has a more accurate calendar than we do. A pity they couldn't be more precise about what they were expecting in 2012 and - more importantly - how to avoid or prevent it. Or maybe they were, but the Conquistadores burned almost all their manuscripts so we are left in the dark. Moctezuma's real revenge. Well, never mind, we could suggest a few scenarios:

'Wasn't that book *The Mayan Prophesies* all about sun spot activity?'

'Maybe they saw another asteroid out in space and charted its course and guess what - it's due back in 2012.'

'Or maybe they reckoned the new ice age will start then?'

'No, no that's not sexy enough. Say they hid these really toxic and undetectable chemicals in the walls of the pyramids and in 2012, they will reactivate with sun spot activity and spread a deadly plague throughout the world.'

'That's ridiculous.'

Well at least it will be a talking point. We can see there will be discussions well into the night on this one.

While at Dzibilchaltún, we could also visit the Xlacah cenote on one corner of the site. This is a large shaded pool that acts as a lido for the local village. However there aren't any depth markings as no one knows how deep it is or how far underground it goes.

The guide books always talk about taking a refreshing dip in any handy cenote; this is really a polite way of saying the water is pretty damn cold. And you may be sharing it with inquisitive little fish that like taking nips to see what you taste like. However, the cenotes are here thanks to the Chicxulub asteroid so we have a handy way to tie our two themes together.

'Now, for day two of the tour.' Martin is really warming to the theme.

'Day two?'

'Well, yes, otherwise they might not want accommodation.'

'Right.'

'OK, so on day two, we are going south to Tecoh to visit the Tzabnah caves to see the rock formations created by the meteorite. There's a huge cave the size of a cathedral; we'll get a really good feel for the geology as we walk through. Plus apparently a Mayan prince and princess get lost down there and are still wandering around.'

'Well I hope we don't get lost and are still wandering around in five hundred years' time. It will not be good publicity for the tour.'

'You take a guide anyway so that shouldn't be a problem. We'll just have to make sure no one wanders off. Then next stop will be Mayapan. We can have a picnic lunch there - we'll have the place to ourselves unless it's suddenly become much more popular.'

Mayapan was the last of the great Mayan cities, with its heyday from 1200 to 1450, after Uxmal and Chichén Itzá went into decline. It is also supposed to be the size of Chichén Itzá although most of it still has to be excavated.

But the pyramids and buildings around the central courtyard have recently been revealed and these include an observatory, like the one at Chichén Itzá, with a circular room at the top. When we last visited, it had been the most atmospheric and peaceful site we'd come across.

'After lunch, we can go and look at the observatory. I am thinking that the evening before, we can do a talk on Mayan astronomy so it makes more sense when we get there.'

Yes, we could get something going here.

Vibrant architecture - lots of ticks. In fact, we can stop trying now.

On the way home from Mayapan, we see a sign for the *Hacienda Teya* - this is just on the eastern outskirts of Mérida and is run as a restaurant and function venue.

'We could take the group there as a treat after the tour.' suggests Martin. I can hear his stomach rumbling.

'So I think we should try it out now.'

'I totally agree.'

We turn off the main road, through a small village and into the grand gates of *Hacienda Teya.*

'This is going to set the budget back big time.'

'Well, we can put it down to research for our business.'

'Right.'

Like several of the old Haciendas around Mérida and on the way to Campeche, this one has been lovingly restored and turned into a business.

Most of the others are now very exclusive hotels with huge rooms full of original furniture (including, of course, plenty of rocking chairs), tranquil pools and top-class restaurants. The *Teya* is primarily a restaurant - the kind of place people came for business meals and family dos. An ornate orangery in the grounds serves as a venue for large wedding receptions and parties.

Today, at around two-thirty on a weekday, it does not seem that busy. A large number of waiters in smart white jackets are hanging around the entrance. There is some competition for our custom. Menus came at us from all directions. The winner leads us triumphantly through a large dining room to a table at the end.

As we settle at our table and the waiter goes to fetch drinks, we take a surreptitious look around. The other diners are fairly smartly dressed. We are sweaty and crumpled from scrambling around Mayapan.

'I think we're lowering the tone.'

'Don't worry; just act nonchalant,' advises Martin, flicking his napkin open.

'I don't think I can, seeing the prices on this menu.'

'Well, we can have a treat once in a while.'

Martin orders a Yucatecan platter with a sample of all his favourite dishes: cochinita pibil, enchiladas con mole, poc chuc. I try their spicy dogfish empanadas.

The food is good even if it feels a little production line; as if the kitchen is more used to preparing for two hundred, not two.

But we still give it two ticks.

Beneath the restaurant there is a shop selling locally produced liqueurs and honey and fairly pricey little gifts. Still, this is somewhere our tour members can buy their more upmarket presents to take home.

'Maybe that's the way to make money: do up an old hacienda?' I suggest on our way home.

The real estate agents usually have several ruined haciendas on their books. These rambling properties have deserted machine rooms where the henequen was processed to produce tough natural fibre. Beautiful tumble down façades with bell towers and crumbling terraces invite you to rescue them.

It's not surprising that local people have a slightly ambivalent attitude to these places. They are, after all, the equivalent almost of slave plantations where the owners lived in luxury while the workers laboured away, kept permanently in debt by having to use the estate shop to buy over-priced food. At their height in the early twentieth century, a large number of Korean workers were brought in to bolster the workforce on the Haciendas and their descendants are now fully settled here.

'Don't even consider it. We've got enough on our plate with a mini-hacienda. Anyway, those places start at several hundred thousand. Plus there's enough competition at that top end of the market already.'

'I am thinking more of running a kind of do-it-yourself honey and fruit farm for stressed out celebrities. We'll have a 'get your hands dirty to get back to reality' kind of approach.

Martin is not convinced. 'Let's just concentrate on getting the B & B up and running.'

'OK.'

As an alternative to going to *Hacienda Teya*, we could offer a day trip to one of the haciendas that has been turned into a working museum, showing how the whole place would have operated in its heyday.

Even if the tour is shaping up, we still have work to do to get everything up and running. The apartments don't have any furniture and we really are avoiding buying it too soon before we open as Emily has put pressure on the budget. Not that we've been spending wildly. But if you've got no income, someday the money's going to run out. We have a few ground rules. Never ever go into:

- A coffee shop.
- A juice bar.
- Any clothes shop.
- Any shoe shop.
- Any American fast-food chain - no not even if you really feel you need a burger.

The good news is…

- You can go to the cinema on Mondays when it's a special price (three dollars each) though in fact we've only been to the cinema once.
- A maximum of two meals out a week and not more than 10 dollars a trip.
- Use cheap, fresh ingredients from the market for cooking. Cook-chill ready meals don't exist as a concept here anyway - just as well.
- Use shampoo instead of shower gel, which is hard to find and comparatively expensive, as most people here use soap.
- Chips only on special occasions, even from the stall by the university (a portion anywhere here is more expensive than the local chippie in the UK).
- Borrow English language books from the Mérida English Library instead of buying them at extortionate prices.
- No copies of Mexican *Elle*, *Vogue* or Spanish *¡Hola!* etc. etc. All those Iberian royals are dead boring anyway.
- No imported goods - apart that is from chocolate, which is an allowable exception.

Not surprising, then, we are addicted to the American TV show *Lost*, watching the survivors stranded on the remote island make do without all life's little luxuries…and staying remarkably well dressed and clean.

Watching *Lost* loses us most of our ticks for genuine culture - although it does have plenty of dramatic scenery going for it.

We must be doing something right - every time we go back to the UK, people tell us how well we are looking. Now whether this is code for: 'You total slacker' or not, we don't care.

Hey, we can't exactly complain. It's not a bad life being able to take a dip in the pool whenever you feel like it, read as many books as you want and take a siesta in the afternoon. Though old habits are hard to kick and we usually get up at seven to do the pool before it gets hot and only really take siestas if we are ill or have been working very hard on the decorating. Is this a sad waste of time or what?

So, we might not have any furniture yet for the apartments but we do want to plan the décor. One day, we go looking for inspiration on one of the weekly Mérida house tours launched from the English Library. This takes in three or four houses not usually open to the public, and, it has to be said, mainly foreign owned. Yucatecan families are intensely private and aren't keen on having tourists traipse through their living room - unless they are planning on selling.

Number one on our tour can really claim to be historic as it was the home of Felipe Carillo Puerto, a reforming Governor of the Yucatán who was assassinated for his efforts in 1924. We've often passed the façade without another look at its slightly peeling paint as we negotiate the narrow pavement. Like all the houses in Centro, inside is another story.

From the road, you will never realise how extensive many of the houses are. Usually the entrance room covers the whole of the width of the lot, and then opens onto a set of reception rooms that lead to a colonnaded courtyard, with the bedrooms arranged along one side. The high ceilings and interconnecting rooms are designed to maximise airflow.

The only problem being that in the old days you could leave all the windows onto the street open, and put an iron gate across instead of closing the heavy wooden front door during the day. That plan went wrong when cars replaced horses and started bombing along the narrow streets.

Out in the courtyard garden, there is a pool and a windmill to pump water from the well that is still in use. In the old days, every house had one.

Martin looks at it dubiously.

'That thing will crash straight onto the roof in the next hurricane. What's the problem with electricity?'

'Well you're more self-reliant with a windmill. The electricity always goes off if a hurricane hits.'

'Yes but the windmill will have crashed anyway. So that's a lot of use.'

The garden also has a circular bar made by cutting the top half off a massive old water cistern. This is another way that people used to get their water - all the run off from the roofs was stored. You can still see them in the backyards of many older houses, including the old mansion next door to ours.

The next house is run as a B & B. Ha. We pay close attention. Huh: their pool is not really swimmable; more for dips, although it does have a fantastic cascading fountain. The sound of gushing water is lovely and cooling. They also have a beautiful tiled breakfast area where you can sit on a long bench that curves around the wall. Plus it is roofed so there is no need to evacuate when it rains.

But, but, but - they have mini packets of cereals on the help-yourself-bar. Oh dear. We've read in our UK B & B books that mini packs of cornflakes and puffed rice are really not on. However they know their North American clientele better than we do. Then Martin takes me aside and whispers:

'Did you hear him talk lovingly about the lawn? Call that a lawn? It's not even three foot square. I could show him a lawn.'

'Yes, though I bet it doesn't need 40 minutes of watering every night.'

'That is not the point. It's pure tokenism. Also, the guest rooms look dark.'

'We haven't been into the guest rooms.'

'Well I can see from here. And they're poky.'

'No you can't: you're just jealous. And everything is really well finished. The decoration is beautiful. You can't imagine they have any problems with malfunctioning sewage systems.'

'Want a bet?'

In the owner's quarters, we can hear everyone else getting really excited by 'gorgeous' balls in the bathroom. We get worried until we see they are stone balls - bigger than canon balls and apparently *the* must have item to be in with any chance of making the grade in house styling. And preferably, they should be ancient stone balls.

And there is also the interesting detail of a wrought-iron staircase that doesn't lead anywhere.

I nudge Martin.

'Am I being dense here? That staircase just goes into the wall.'

'I can't work it our either.'

We are obviously just not up to the mark on house design. We need to do something urgently: this is the city where all the new, design-led hotels have websites that play plangent guitar music and display close-up pictures of exotic flowers, flowing fountains and billowing curtains - and maybe a small picture of a bedroom as an after thought.

'It's called mood, I think.' I remark.

'Well I call it something else,' declares Martin, 'websites should give you information first and foremost.'

'But here, you really have to get the edge somehow.'

It is time to move on to the last house.

This is yet another mansion hiding behind - to be honest - a really dingy façade. Our tour leader explains that the city council has a system of grants and permissions to paint the façades in Centro. However there are often disputes because they have their own idea about what should be done that is not always what the owner wants. And this can go on for years.

So the houses go unpainted. As our house does not have a façade straight on the street and is not an old colonial, at least we don't have that problem. So we can paint it all colours of the rainbow. And that's exactly what we have done.

This house has an amazing mural all around the dining room wall, showing busy scenes in the actual streets and squares that surround the house, and then further out, all the Mayan sites beyond the city with the pyramids and other buildings accurately depicted. Plus we love the kitchen, colourfully tiled on every surface possible, which would send lovers of black granite into a real tizzy.

Out the back there is a very stylish pool. One side - well actually most of it - is a series of shallow, wide steps with above them hammocks strung over the water. Martin is whispering in my ear again.

'That is not a swimming pool. I don't know what it is but you can't swim in it.'

'You know, I'm beginning to get the idea that you're not really supposed to swim in pools here. It's not, like, stylistically cool. It's more a concept of water and relaxation you need to be aiming for.'

'This tour is getting to you. Good thing it's nearly over.'

At least we can now add more ticks for vibrant architecture - other people's, if not our own place.

On the way home we pass a house very close to ours where a huge team of workmen has been hard at work for several months, even slinging their hammocks there at night. Through the open window, we can see they are putting in replica decorative pasta tiles on the floors, moulding a beautiful kitchen with an ornate canopy over the oven, fitting carved wooden doors and shutters. There is a very superior real estate agent's sign hanging outside. We rush back to check the internet.

'350 thousand dollars? That's ridiculous.'

'And look at this. You cross a bridge over the 'mirror pool' to get to the master bedroom. What happens if you've had too many marguerites?'

'Well you won't drown, judging by the pools we've seen today.'

'At least it's only got three bedrooms so it can't be a hotel.'

We are developing an envy problem here. It is getting really disheartening:

- One, our pool is dead uncool. Also, the closest we have to a fountain is when we stick the hose over the side and pump water out of the well to top the pool up.

- Two, we do not have a lawn with attitude, just masses of grass full of mosquitoes.

- Three, there are stones in random heaps in the two far corners of our garden but they are not ball shaped and no one in their right mind could claim they are making a design statement.

- Four, very critically, we have an upstairs. This really lets us down. It's acceptable to have internal stairs as a feature - just as long as they don't go anywhere. Guest rooms should be entered from a courtyard, preferably crossing a bridge over a pool.

But wait a minute: external staircases with ornate railings leading to guest rooms with balconies might just be alright. And we do have an external staircase leading to the upper apartment.

Right, all is not lost. We have to think: Transformation and we can still do it. We just have to keep saying to ourselves: mood, ambience, mood, ambience.

'Look,' says Martin, 'we can put a small fountain into the wall in the front courtyard. People will come in through the door in the gates and think: wow.'

'As long as they don't bump their head on the way in.' We've had a door put into the gates so you don't have to open them up every time you go in and out. But the door is fitted to the average height of the locals - at just over five foot I am fine. Anyone much taller has to stoop.

Martin is really getting into the transformation:

'At the back, we can create a colonnaded courtyard with another fountain in the middle. At the same time, this will give us balconies for all the bedrooms. Plus, we can turn the service room at the back into another ground floor guest suite.'

'You don't think we're getting carried away here?' I try not to remind him that I suggested all this some time ago and got a short answer.

'Well if we want to attract business, we have to compete. Plus, it will look more colonial, which will make it easier to sell if things don't work out.'

'In that case, we'll have to do something about the inside as well.'

All this is going to cost more money. And we are still paying out several hundred pounds a month to keep our UK house going - council tax, utility charges, caretaking, gardening - it is all adding up. Crunch point is approaching, very fast.

'Look', says Martin, 'there's not much point in doing anything until the hurricane season is over. We don't want to do building work here and then get hit. Let's wait until the beginning of November, this will still give us time as the main tourist season doesn't start until just before Christmas.'

OK, we are putting it off again. But we've already been hit in Akumal and then New Orleans was devastated by Katrina. The one laugh in all this is when the Mexican army sends a detachment to help out in New Orleans. This is the first time Mexican troops have been allowed onto US soil since the last war between the two countries, donkey's years ago. All the Mexican papers show the troop lorries crossing the border and proclaim triumphantly:

'Mexico invades America!'

That feels good.

Otherwise, this hurricane season is turning into a nightmare. If Mérida takes a hit, it will be goodbye to tourists for a while. So it makes sense to hold off longer.

'Well, let's at least do some of the trips we've been promising ourselves. Come on, let's get the bus down to the ruins at Palenque.'

Wow, this should mean a tick for everything on my list.

- Dramatic scenery.
- Vibrant architecture.
- Amazing wildlife.
- Vivid colours.
- Incredible contrasts.
- Fantastic customs.

- Real Mexican food.
- Genuine culture.
- Local forms of transport.
- Everyday life.
- The beauty of it all.

But then again, maybe we're getting tired of lists. Perhaps we should just relax and not try so hard from now on.

Chapter 11: Palenque here we come!

We've promised ourselves for months that we will one day take a trip down south to the Palenque ruins in Chiapas state. All the guidebooks have photos of the pyramids rising out of the Lacandon rain forest, shrouded in mist. Ah, we think, this is how ruins are supposed to be: remote, deserted, atmospheric.

It isn't exactly the best time to go. We are into October and Hurricane Stan has just dumped a huge amount of rain on southern Chiapas and neighbouring Guatemala so that rivers have swollen and flooded, there've been landslides and houses and bridges washed away. Palenque is north of the worst affected area and reports say the town is fine and the ruins are open for business as usual.

So we book our tickets on the long-distance ADO bus. The journey time is about seven and a half hours. This means there will be time for a least three videos. The posh ADO GL buses that run on some routes even have separate gents and ladies' toilets, extra large seats and a hostess trolley with free beverages waiting for you as you board. All the buses have GPS tracking and an alarm that sounds if the driver goes over the permitted speed limit - even by a fraction. Sitting at the front, you won't have much sleep as the drivers listen to Mariachi and other up-tempo beats to keep their concentration.

We've taken the bus on the four and a half hour journey to and from the Caribbean coast a number of times at a cost of about sixteen dollars a go.

By now we've seen *Garfield* twice, *Hero* three times, *Spanglish* four times (this is about a Mexican mother and daughter who immigrate to the States. We sympathise with mom's desperate attempts to learn English, feeling the same way about Spanish). The other films are the kind you used to borrow from the video shop on a wet Sunday evening when all the good films had already been rented. All the same, if they're in Spanish, this is good for us and if they have sub titles, this is even better as we can improve our vocabulary *and* understand what is going on at the same time.

The bus leaves around eight in the morning and heads down towards Campeche on the Gulf coast. Pirates used to treat the town as their local cash and carry (except they always forgot to pay) for more than two hundred years until in 1668 everyone got fed up with being raided and built a wall around the town. Now it is a UN World Heritage site with all the old colonial houses lovingly restored.

We are planning to stop off here on our return journey. This means we will probably have to eat fish as there doesn't seem to be anything else on offer in the town's restaurants. People travel here especially for the ceviche (lime-marinated raw seafood), so we ought to give it a try.

Our bus driver is really friendly - he waves to all the ADO drivers going the other way, any other bus line drivers, even truck drivers. The only ones he doesn't wave to are gringo tour buses but we only pass a couple of them. As we head on past Campeche, we settle down to watch *Garfield* again. We are getting really tired of that smug cat. This is only after we have seen the safety video reminding us to fasten our seat belts and be very quick if we want to use the WC on the journey in case of bad corners (or, more likely, someone else getting desperate due to the freezing cold air conditioning).

After passing through a number of fishing villages, the bus heads away from the coastline. The weather is deteriorating rapidly - overcast, drizzly, just like most days in the UK in fact - except the rain is getting heavier by the minute. With the amount of surface water, our driver is taking things carefully. Every couple of hours, we have a scheduled stop for ten minutes at a bus station.

'Right,' says Martin, jumping up as the bus pulls in, 'let's get outside to warm up.' So we go out and mooch around in the humid rain, and watch other passengers rummaging around in their cases in the hold, in the forlorn hope they might just have something warm to wear in there.

'I wish I'd brought a jumper,' says Martin wistfully. 'You don't expect to need a woolly in Mexico in August. I'll have to wear my plastic rain coat. Better than nothing.'

We look around for any vendors selling something warm - wool jackets or even a nice hot tea. Not a hope and we don't have time to go wandering into a strange town.

At each stop, a guy will appear with a bucket and cleaning materials and check out the on board WC. Another orderly, standing on a stepladder, will give the windscreen a thorough clean. Sometimes, if you are lucky, someone will come on board with a tray of fresh-baked hojaldras. Otherwise, there will be a rush for the station kiosk to buy crisps, biscuits and drinks. Amazing how the cold makes you hungry.

For the last part of the journey, we are passing through a rural scenery of hedged fields and cattle grazing. We almost feel we are back in the English countryside - except the trees look strange and the cattle are more like buffaloes. It is seriously disorientating. At our last stop, Emiliano Zapata, we look down from the bus station car park at the huge swollen river, grey and threatening. We're glad there aren't any rivers back in the Yucatán.

'At this rate, we'll have the site to ourselves', says Martin.

'That's if we can get to it. We're supposed to be there by now'.

About an hour later, the bus finally arrives in the town of Palenque (real name Santo Domingo, though no one seems to use that anymore). We are in for a shock. We had been imagining that Palenque would be in the middle of nowhere, that there would be virtually no tourists, and we would wander through the misty, romantic ruins all by ourselves. Some chance!

Shouldering our rucksacks, we walk up the town's steep hill to the main square. On the way we hear German, French, Italian, Dutch and British English. The one accent we don't hear is American. Later we find out that the US State Department warns against travel to Chiapas. Despite this, there are plenty of tourists from the rest of the world. The town is really bustling. And the prices in the restaurants are higher than in Mérida.

On our walk through town, we notice a couple of families of Lacandon Indians with their distinctive long black hair - both men and women. In the rain forest they live by hunting and wear simple white shifts. However, modern-day pressures are taking their toll; people are moving to the towns to get work.

We can hear someone making a speech over a loud speaker in the main square and hurry to see what is going on.

A big truck, heavily laden, is waiting outside the municipal offices. A dignitary is conducting a formal send off. The truck contains donations and relief supplies from the town for the people affected by the floods further south in Chiapas. Everyone starts waving and clapping as it sets off with a couple of police pick-ups, full of garrafons of drinking water, as escorts. We feel definitely frivolous, doing the tourist thing.

'But' argues Martin 'if tourists stay away, it will make things worse. This town obviously depends on tourism and everything is OK here. In fact, we'd better find somewhere to stay quick, as there are so many tourists.'

We decide to take a taxi down the road that leads from the town out to the Mayan ruins. The guide books list a number of hotels here. Some of them come with a health warning. This is a backpackers' Mecca and *the* place to bring your drums and well… drum for hours, in fact all night if you feel like it. That is very nice if you like drumming. But we had this vision of staying somewhere peaceful in the middle of the rainforest.

'Do you think these places are open?'

You obviously need to be in the know to tell which turning to take for your chosen hotel, and even to tell whether it is still operating. Some of them look pretty ramshackle. In Mexico you never know: they can turn out to be deluxe eco-cabañas.

'To hell with it, let's go to the *Chan-Kah*'

According to the guide books, this hotel had cabins in the forest and a lagoon-like pool. The downside is it hosts regular conferences and conventions so it may be packed out. It is also comparatively pricey but travellers' reviews on the web say, if you ask nicely, there are some cabins without a/c further away from the restaurant and other amenities that are cheaper.

We obviously don't ask nicely as the receptionist denies all knowledge of rooms at a cheaper rate. Still, for a couple of nights it is not expensive by UK standards. So we decide to treat ourselves. And it is also close to the ruins - we will be able to pick up a colectivo van out on the road early tomorrow and get to the ruins before anyone else. Maybe we can still have them to ourselves.

That evening we sit out on the terrace of our cabin as the sun goes down and watch giant butterflies flit by. We are admiring the huge ceiba trees. Sacred to the ancient Maya, they grow very tall with thick trunks and elongated roots all entwined above ground forming a root wigwam at the base of the tree.

'It's so peaceful here', I say, 'I'm glad we didn't stay in the town. Bloody hell, what is that?'

An echoing roar is coming out of the trees that surround the cabin.

I make for the door.

'I'm not staying out here. That sounded like a lion or something.'

'They don't have lions on this continent.' Martin is standing on the edge of the terrace, trying to see what it is. I am hiding inside the room behind the door.

'Get back in here quickly. It might be a jaguar. They definitely have those here. There's that model of a two-headed one at Uxmal. Now that will be really scary. Quick, come inside.'

'No. I'm going to have a look. Want to come? Or are you too scared?'

'All right, I'm coming with you. In case it attacks while you're gone'

'It's not going to attack, OK!'

'I'm not convinced, I think we'd better take a weapon or something for when it comes for us.'

'We haven't got anything…wow that is loud.'

'And closer. Look, I'm taking the umbrella. I can always ram it into its mouth when it pounces.'

'If you don't hurry up, we'll miss it.'

'Good!'

Martin hurries off down the path into the gathering gloom. Reluctantly, I trot after him brandishing the umbrella.

We can hear a thrashing noise coming from high up in the trees.

'I'm sure it's a jaguar, up in one of the ceiba trees.'

'Oh no, it's coming this way.'

A huge roar vibrates through the dusk from a tree just above us.

'Hey, I saw its tail.'

'Let's get out of here.'

'It's a monkey!'

'A monkey can't roar like that. The jaguar must be coming after it.'

'No, listen, it is the monkey making that noise.'

'How can it? It's not big enough.'

'It's a howler monkey, that's why!'

'Doesn't sound like howling to me.'

'Quick, you stay here and watch where it goes. I want to record it. Strangest howl I've ever heard.'

'We can pretend it is a jaguar.' I suggest.

'Listen, there are no jaguars around here. Full stop. You can relax, OK?'

'Not if that din goes on all night.'

Fortunately it does not, and we are up bright and early to get a good start at the ruins. When the colectivo drops us at the entrance, we are in for a shock. It is only eight and the car park already has several coaches in it. Groups of tourists are converging on the ticket office.

'Where have all these people come from? They can't all have been staying around here, can they? There was hardly anyone in the restaurant last night.'

'Maybe they all flew in to that airfield we passed in the bus.'

OK, it isn't as busy as Chichén Itzá, but, when all the pictures you have seen show one, or at the most, two isolated figures standing in a deserted site, then it comes as a shock to find you are not alone, not by a long way.

As at all the major sites, there is a group of professional guides at the entrance waiting to be hired. We decide to rely on our book instead. Later we realise we have missed out as the Mexican guides have to go through rigorous training, speak several languages fluently and have information you can't find in the tourist books.

As we follow the crowds into the site, it is still misty and even a little chilly. Palenque is in the foothills of the Chiapas Highlands, whose main town San Cristóbal de las Casas, can get very cold: the houses need heating more than air-conditioning.

Palenque is one of the sites re-discovered and publicised by American explorer John Lloyd Stephens in the mid-nineteenth century. We have copies of the incredibly detailed drawings made by Englishman Frederick Catherwood who accompanied the expeditions. They had to hack their way through the jungle to get to the sites, which were half buried under the tropical growth. Even now, most of the sites have not been fully excavated. You can stand at a high point at Uxmal and see at least two pyramids that are still covered in trees and undergrowth.

At Palenque, the best secret of the site was only found by accident in 1952 in real *Indiana Jones* style. This is in the Temple of the Inscriptions, which rises steeply on the right as you go into the site. Archaeologist Alberto Ruz was standing at the top of the pyramid when he spotted notches in a floor slab and found it was designed to be levered up. Underneath was a staircase going down through the interior of the pyramid to a chamber at ground level. On the way down, he found several skeletons - not early explorers who got trapped, but more likely they were sacrificial victims.

Inside a stone sarcophagus was a body with an amazing jade mask.

This is thought to have been Pakal who was Palenque's ruler in the seventh century and built many of the temples and pyramids. However, some people claim it isn't Pakal at all but an extra-terrestrial who got stuck and, unlike ET, couldn't get home. This is because the relief on the top of the stone coffin looks like an astronaut if you stretch your imagination.

Martin's parents toured around Mexico some twenty-five years ago when even Chichén Itzá was pretty quiet. At Palenque, they had been able to roam at will and descend into Pakal's tomb. Now only bona fide archaeologists are allowed down there. You can't even climb to the top. And the mask has been taken to Mexico City, although there's a replica in the site museum. Instead, you can admire the tomb of Alberto Ruz, a modest stone affair. Unlike ET he obviously didn't want to go home.

The best building now for exploring is the palace in the middle of the site. We climb up to the top and I am intrigued by some steps going down into the centre.

'Come on, let's have a look down there. Maybe it's another tomb.'

'No, it's just dark and smelly, let's go on and look at the inscriptions in the main courtyard.'

'Well I'm going down, bye!'

At the bottom, a passageway disappears into the distance.

'Hey, this is good, come and have a look, Indiana.'

Narrow openings let light into the passageway, which makes several turns and opens out into larger chambers with stone tables in them.

Martin appears.

'Well I'm glad we found this.'

More than anything else here, it gives you a feel for how it must have been to live or, more likely, work in the palace. No doubt you spent your days scurrying around the passageways, only emerging to serve the nobles food or do their bidding. And making sure you stayed off the next sacrificial hit list.

We come out by the central courtyard, which is just like a colonnaded villa with an empty pool in the middle and some nice carvings all around it.

'Hey', exclaims Martin, 'I've got an idea. Forget colonial. Let's do a Mayan style makeover. It's easy to get copies of the reliefs - they'll go around the garden walls. We'll have a Chac-Mool reclining statue by the pool and stone benches. But no stone balls, definitely not.'

The rest of the site is getting quite busy, so we divert along a narrow path that eventually leads to a waterfall and rapids.

'Peace at last. I can't believe all these tourists.'

'So what does that make us?'

'Well at least we're not day trippers on a package.'

'Er, right.'

Not only are there plenty of tourists, there are also several school parties, all smartly dressed in their school uniforms. The girls' uniform is almost always a plaid kilt, mainly a maroon colour - who says Scotland has the monopoly on tartan?

All over the site, the local traders have laid out blankets covered in punched or painted leather: wall hangings, bags and belts. There are also more woolly cats and frogs. I restrain myself.

We climb the final group of smaller pyramids and then head out.

'Maybe it's quieter in the evening' says Martin wistfully.

It is still a mystery how everyone gets there. The coach parties must have come from somewhere. Maybe they've been staying in Villahermosa, where there is a park full of ancient Olmec sculptures of giant heads.

The hotel is still as quiet. We have the huge lagoon pool almost to ourselves - and the howler monkeys.

We have to be up early again to catch the only bus of the day back to Campeche. It is even colder than the one coming down.

'Martin, is that your teeth chattering?'

'I'm never going to survive this all the way back to Mérida.'

'I thought we were going to stay overnight in Campeche anyway?'

'We'll have to now, or I'll freeze to death. You're fine; you've got a cardigan.'

'You can borrow it if you like.'

'No thanks, I'll survive.'

We must have become dehydrated from the a/c on the bus because we misread our map and head the wrong way out of the Campeche bus station. We stop to ask the way and find we had walked a kilometre out of town. Martin pulls out the map.

'I think they must have moved the bus station. According to this map, if the bus station is here, we are in the central square.'

'If we are, someone's done a wonderful job talking it up, that's all I can say. Let's get a taxi.'

'Have you seen any go past? I haven't.'

About an hour later, we finally make it to the central square. Somehow, we aren't feeling that keen on Campeche.

Martin checks the guide book.

'I've just realised something.'

'We are in Campeche, I hope?'

'Yes but today is Monday.'

'And?'

'All the museums are closed on a Monday.'

The other thing to know about Campeche is that it is not really on the coast. They had to build the walls away from the sea front to make it harder for the pirates. So there are no sea views from the old town, unless you go up and walk around the ramparts. However this is Monday, so they are closed.

At the tourist information office, which is just about open although they are having their lunch out the back, we pick up a new map.

'Look,' Martin is triumphant, 'what did I say? They *have* moved the bus station, all the way out here.'

Phew, our self-esteem is intact. The map is wrong, not us.

We wander outside the town walls to the sea front. Since the town got its UN protection, it's been restored inside the walls but down by the sea it is not attractive. There are a couple of really nondescript hotels and a dual carriageway. There isn't even a beach - just a rough sea slapping against the concrete sea defences. We sit and watch it a while.

'I suppose we'd better go and have some fish.' says Martin.

Back in the old town, we find a restaurant with waitresses dressed in colourful skirts. It is filling up fast with local people on working lunches and - ominously - about six tables are reserved for a tour group.

'Why can't we ever get away from these damn tourists?' exclaims Martin.

I look down at our rucksacks and our crumpled clothes.

'Well let's hurry up and order before they turn up.'

We decide to go for - seafood salad. It arrives just as a large and animated French tourist party troop into the restaurant. Martin ladles on a mayonnaise dressing, avoiding comment. The seafood tastes good and fresh.

After lunch, we walk around some more. The old colonial houses are definitely in better shape here than in Mérida. One old house has been restored and room-settings recreated from its heyday in the early twentieth century. At least the heat meant people didn't clutter their rooms up as much as the Edwardians back in the UK. We wander into the colonnaded courtyard. There is a tea shop but today is Monday - so it is closed.

In the central square, a tourist train is waiting to pull carriages on a tour of the old town. The ticket kiosk is all shuttered up.

'Look, I'll go and find some ice cream while we wait.' I volunteer.

Ice cream shops are in short supply. I find one corner shop that has a freezer but hardly any ice creams and they look like they have been there a few years.

I return to Martin sitting disconsolately on the park bench.

'Sorry, no ice creams. But look what I did find!'

I hand over a bag with a long-sleeved sweatshirt in it.

'It was in a sale, only 39 pesos. So we can head home tonight if we want.'

'We do want,' says Martin. While I've been off on the trail of ice cream, the ticket office for the train has opened up. However, they are only going to run if they get eight or more takers. So far they have five including us if we go. We look around. It is unlikely any more passengers are about to appear. Where is that French tour group when we need them?

'Sod it, let's do Campeche another time.'

We head back to the bus station - without getting lost on the way. Then we find that the next bus doesn't leave for ninety minutes.

'I'm going to see if I can find some ice creams.' I am determined to crack this ridiculous ice cream shortage.

The shop in the bus station only sells microwaved burgers. I go over to a petrol station across the road. No ice creams.

When I get back, Martin is looking agitated. In fact he is literally hopping up and down.

'Quick, have you got any small change? I need the loo urgently and you can't get in without paying. It must have been that mayonnaise.'

Fortunately I do have some small coins. Martin grabs them and runs off. At least the loos are modern and well looked after, this being a new bus station.

I abandon the idea of ice cream.

The bus back is not nearly as cold. In fact, Martin has to pull his sweatshirt off half way back to Mérida as he is *too hot.*

One day, we will muster up courage to go back to Campeche and do it properly. There's also the Mayan site of Edzná not far away, with a special bus going twice a day. Next time, we'll take cheese sandwiches. That should be safe enough.

Chapter 12: Here we go again

Immediately we arrive back from Campeche, Martin logs on to check the state of a tropical depression that was starting to form when we set out on our expedition.

It has now strengthened to a tropical storm and acquired a name: Wilma.

'It's a cert it's going to turn into a hurricane,' says Martin. 'And it's heading our way. There's a possibility it might go up the channel between the Yucatán and Cuba. I wouldn't bet on it.'

'Akumal's going to get hit again, isn't it?'

'Probably. What's more, Cancun is right in Wilma's path unless they are very lucky. That's going to be major if they take a hit.'

By the next day, Wilma has become a hurricane and we have an email from Roberto. Yes, just as everything had got back to normal after Emily, it is about to start all over again.

'We're feeling like Groundhog Day here. The guests are being evacuated. We're making preparations. I'm staying.'

And Morrison is too, it goes without saying. The regular crew is all ready.

It is very unlikely that Wilma will cut across the Yucatán to Mérida, but the whole of the Riviera Maya, including the island of Cozumel just off Playa, is in her path and also the eastern most section of the Gulf coastline.

The familiar hurricane alert ditty is playing on the radio and TV again.

There are scenes from Cancun airport of tourists besieging the airline desks, trying to get a flight out. The main hotel zone in Cancun is on a long, narrow spit of land directly fronting the sea. This is going to be very vulnerable if Wilma strikes the coast. And all the predictions are she is going to turn into a category five, the most powerful and dangerous.

By Thursday night, all the tourists left in Cancun have to go to hurricane shelters. Coastal resorts like Akumal have been evacuated and people in fishing villages on the Gulf coast are bussed to shelters. Conditions might be rough and ready but you can't accuse the Mexican authorities of abandoning people to fend for themselves, like in New Orleans when Katrina struck earlier in the season.

Everyone is still hoping that somehow, Wilma will miss the coast.

In Mérida, things are carrying on more or less as normal although an amber alert is in force. Tourists are streaming in from the coast. We don't have any furniture for our apartments and they aren't really ready to take guests.

Later, we go around to see Dan and Sofi: they say people had been besieging them for rooms and wouldn't have minded sleeping in hammocks. We ask them to tell anyone that they can stay in our place for free as it will be pretty basic, although the showers work at least; and we rush back to sling our spare hammocks and make the apartments as presentable as possible.

Great timing: if only we'd got our apartments ready before, we could have offered proper accommodation and maybe kick-started ourselves into finally opening for business.

Martin stands surveying the top apartment:

- Two single beds cobbled together from various bases and mattresses that Lucia has stored with us.
- Bedside tables and lamps.
- One plastic table.
- Two dining chairs with cushions.

That's the lot.

'No one's going to want to stay here, even if they don't have to pay.'

'Why not? In a hotel, you don't get much more. Plus this is a very big room and there's a kitchen. With proper furniture it will be great. You know what our problem is?'

'Right now, I don't know what our problem *isn't*.'

'We just need to think positive. When Wilma's over, we've just got to go for it.'

'When Wilma's over, we may not have much left to go with if Akumal gets hit again, which looks a total certainty.'

Probably not the best time to get all enthusiastic.

To be honest, we feel pretty glum and powerless and spend most of the time on the internet, checking the projections for Wilma. It really is like a bad dream when you see a train in the distance and know it is going to crash but you can't do anything about it. Except that a category five hurricane is much more powerful than a train.

From Friday onwards Wilma starts churning her way up the coast. Mérida is on red alert because the east part of Yucatán state is in the path. The traffic lights are taken down again and the roads go quiet.

This is when the internet turns into one enormous rumour city. Telephone lines have all gone down over on the Riviera Maya and mobile masts are being taken out like dominoes so the tiniest piece of news coming out is being seized on. Riviera tourist blogs that are usually full of questions about how good is this or that hotel or is this bar still the hip place, are now asking: is this hotel still there? Do you know where people have been evacuated to?

We begin to hate that little word: *gone.*

Blogs keep on being posted reporting the worst:

'*Buena Vida*, Akumal has *gone*.' (This is a restaurant just down the road from our building with a trademark skeleton of a 'sea monster' hanging over the bar).

'Puerto Morelos has *gone*. All the houses, restaurants, hotels on the beach are totally *gone*.'

You don't know what to believe:

'All the crocodiles in the zoo have escaped and disappeared into the mangroves. They are very hungry.'

And some desperate pleas:

'We're due to get married in four days at the *Bahia Principe* hotel, do you think it will be open again by then?'

Over the weekend, Wilma stalls on the tip of the Yucatán, right over Cancun after having done the same thing to Cozumel.

At last on Sunday, we get real news from Akumal: this time, it hasn't been the wind so much as the sea. Wilma pushed a powerful storm surge in front of her so that huge waves pounded the coast for hours.

Roberto later gives us an eye witness account:

'I was running out between the waves. I could hear the water surging right past the office and onto the road. It smashed into the ground floor and all the furniture was hitting the walls and getting sucked out. Wrecked stuff was floating all over the bay: fridges, cookers, tables and chairs, everything. Water was inches deep even in the office. You know, water can blow right through a solid wall if the wind is strong enough. And it was.'

At least there are no reports of fatalities apart from someone who was electrocuted while cutting branches in Playa before the hurricane struck.

The road behind the buildings on the beach has been covered in many feet of debris and sand. The five foot deep swimming pool is so completely full of it you can't tell there is any pool there. Electricity, water and telephones are all out again. The good news is that the *Buena Vida* hasn't really *gone*. The palapa roof has blown away and the structure is battered but there is something still standing. Hooray.

And pretty soon a new sea monster is being 'unearthed' from all the sand, named Wilma and hung above the bar pronto. Who needs a roof - we're back in business guys.

Roberto is the only person who can get into or out of Half Moon Bay for several days as he has a motorcycle that can get over the mounds of debris - ten foot in places - covering the road.

We all need to send money again urgently to start the clear up. The insurance for Emily hasn't come through yet and we wonder if it ever will now.

Meanwhile, by Monday Wilma has finally left Cancun and people are emerging from shelters to a scene of total devastation, like the whole holiday playground has been kicked around by an angry child. The hotels are still standing but are in a badly wrecked state with shattered glass, mangled bits of metal, wiring and everything hanging out like wounded guts. The fantastic coral sand beach has really all gone: pushed over into the lagoon behind the hotels or swept away.

And there is a big problem: both the terminals at the airport have been badly damaged so no commercial airliners will be able to fly out for several days. Roads out of Cancun to Mérida are flooded and impassable. The only way in is up the coastal Highway 307 from Chetumal way down in the south, once that road has been cleared of debris.

Tourists are stuck in the shelters with minimal hygiene but then no one in Cancun has running water or electricity. It is pretty grim and then looting breaks out. This is controlled pretty quickly and some of it could be people just getting desperate for supplies.

The authorities are determined this is not going to turn into another New Orleans, not least because Cancun brings in so much foreign revenue and provides so many jobs: the country cannot afford the crisis to become a disaster. Also, they want to show America how to handle a hurricane properly. So there.

But the tourists are still stuck, waiting desperately at the airport for any plane to get out. However, someone sees an opportunity and vendors are out selling 'I survived Wilma' t-shirts in Cancun. This is a chance for clean clothes *and* a souvenir in one go.

After a couple of days, coaches start getting through the floods and out to Mérida although it is taking sixteen hours and the luggage holds got flooded. Long queues are building up at Mérida airport as people scramble to get on any available flight. There are pictures of people hanging their clothes out to dry on the bushes in front of the airport. The authorities are down there with medical help, food and bedding. We phone a number on the web for offers of accommodation, but don't get any takers. Mostly it seems it is tour groups needing lots of rooms, as independent travellers don't want to leave the airport for fear of missing their place in the queue.

Flights start to get out of Cancun - we hear that British tourists are being flown to the Dominican Republic by their tour companies.

President Fox is promising state aid and electricians and other workers are being drafted in from all over the country to help with the recovery. Businesses on the Riviera are promised tax breaks if they keep on all their workers, even if waiters have to become painters until things are fixed.

The US government announces it is making a donation to help with the clear up: about a hundred thousand dollars. Wow, how generous. Thanks Mr Bush.

Before Wilma appeared on the horizon, Martin had booked a flight out of Cancun to Miami for the coming Thursday to get to his sister's big 50th birthday party. It doesn't seem to be a very good idea to be heading for Cancun right now even if the road is sort of passable and the airport is kind of operating, but the airlines are playing a very slow game. They are only cancelling and refunding scheduled flights on a day-by-day basis, otherwise you can reschedule without a refund.

'Listen, do you really think it's sensible to go to Cancun when everyone else is desperate to get out? If you can get there in the first place. You could be stuck on the toll road for days.'

'It might be OK in a couple of days. And I promised I would try to get back for my sister's do if I can.'

'Remember that film *Trains, Planes and Automobiles*? Do you want a nightmare journey like that?'

'He got home in time in the end.'

Martin reschedules for Saturday and changes his flight out of Miami. On Friday, it is cancelled. Only charter flights are operating, getting the last of the tourists out.

He reschedules for Tuesday, and yes it is cancelled.

After the third reschedule, we head up to the *American Airlines* office off the Paseo. There is already a queue of independent travellers who are trying to find a way home. The one guy in the office is desperately trying to get the computers to work. In the meantime, he is phoning the same number that thousands of other people are trying.

Miami airport is closed. Wilma checked into Florida after leaving Cancun. Flights to Houston from Mérida are all full. The only possibility is to fly to Mexico City and get a flight from there. But other people have thought of that already. Plus it will cost. And you will have to phone direct to buy a ticket. Then you will be very lucky to get one.

We head back home again.

'Why not wait a few weeks and then go? After all, at least you're not desperate to get home like all these other people. And now you've missed your sister's do anyway.'

'But the health insurance only covers 96 days at a go. That's next week. And they won't extend. And knowing our luck, I'll break my back falling off a ladder if I don't go. Plus the house insurance means we can't leave it more than 60 days. And I need to go into the office. And what's more, I'm damned if I'm going to be beaten.'

We give it a few days, then go up to the *Continental* office, and finally get a flight from Mérida to Houston. In the end *American Airlines* give a refund, and *Virgin* only charge once for a change, although by then Martin has rescheduled his Atlantic flight four times.

Back in the 70's, word has it that the Mexican authorities put a whole load of criteria into a computer to come up with the ideal place in Mexico to build a new tourist resort. It came back with Cancun. Maybe the stats on hurricanes got lost. In 1988 Cancun was hit by Hurricane Gilbert and had a few low years, property prices falling, hotel tariffs slashed, before bouncing back.

Even then, no one seems to have twigged that maybe it had a unique vulnerability and it might be a good idea to build another airport closer than Mérida but far enough away that it would not be taken out at the same time as Cancun.

Otherwise the problem with evacuation is going to happen and get worse every time, with tourist numbers rising and more and more hotels going up along the coast. Now the word is, a new airport is going to be built near Tulum, not that far from Akumal. And there will be a new super highway *and* a bullet train. Great, just as long as the next hurricane doesn't hit for ten years.

Mexican TV is running a telethon to raise money for relief - with celebrities manning the phones on screen. The actor who plays Tito in *Los Sánchez* is there doing his bit. But where are his highlights? I think we should know. Maybe he thought they would be too frivolous for the occasion.

In Mérida, donation centres are opened. The requests are very specific: powdered milk, tinned fish, loo roll - and sanitary towels. I've read somewhere that male aid organisers had forgotten (more like were too embarrassed to say anything) about these after the Asian Tsunami appeal so I always put a couple of packets into the bags we take along. One good thing is that the appeal is for victims of Stan as well, as they are claiming they've been forgotten by the federal authorities.

Meanwhile, we want to know if we can help in Akumal. We get in touch with Roberto.

'Are there any owners there at the moment?'

'No, thank god!'

Hurricanes are no sweat compared with a hoard of demanding owners descending on the hotel. The best thing we can do is send money and keep clear while the work goes on.

At least Akumal's beach properties have not suffered as badly as some in Puerto Morelos further north, close to Cancun. Here at least one house has split in two. The front half is now leaning at a steep angle towards the beach, the other half falling back the other way. A loo is jutting out of a gaping bathroom like a bad tooth, and the basin is just about hanging on in there, five metres away across the gap. This was the storm surge again that undermined the foundations. And one thing you can't insure on beach front properties are the foundations.

Hurricanes create other strange phenomena like - the phantom loss adjusters. After a hurricane, you must keep everything that's been damaged - there are piles of fridges, mattresses, cookers and broken furniture outside every property in Akumal - so it can be checked for insurance claims.

Roberto tells us how the first group of loss adjusters had been around, checked everything, taken notes and then disappeared. Then the next week, another lot had turned up.

'Well they didn't know who the first lot were but they weren't working for the insurance company.'

The second lot went around, checked everything, took notes and left.

A few weeks later, the real loss adjusters turned up. Yes, they were definitely from the insurance company. No idea who these others were. Maybe they were chancers looking for an opportunity to pick up extra cash from claimants desperate to get priority for their claim? It's a mystery. It's not exactly like it's a glamorous profession that you would pretend to be in just for kicks. Well I hope not.

The insurers are prioritising Wilma and rumour is that it could be up to two years before all the claims for Emily are settled, if they ever are. What is that about one hurricane every ten years, if you are unlucky? And Jeff Masters and all the hurricane watchers are telling us we are in a period of heightened activity that could last another… ten years. Twenty more direct hits to look forward to? Thanks guys.

Chapter 13: What happened to Margot Ham?

Late October. Martin is in the UK and our plans are still uncertain. Well, what the hell, it's great to be warm, there's plenty of Mérida still to explore, and maybe things will start looking up now.

The hurricane season is now really almost finished (cross fingers), and the recovery from Wilma is well underway. Some places, like Playa, that have not taken such a hit as Cancun, are already reopening for business.

In Cancun, the biggest headache is restoring the beach. President Fox has promised that 80% of the resort will be back up and running for Christmas. Without the beach, it will be hard to attract tourists. And the beach can't be replaced with just any old sand. It has to be fine white coral sand that stays cool underfoot in scorching temperatures and has to be dredged from the sea bed.

First they have to find the best way of getting the sand out of the sea and onto the beach and that is not proving easy. Practically every day *El Diario* has a picture of the beach covered in huge tubes, winches, generators and trucks. But the photos always include a couple of sunbathers in bikinis sitting on the micro beach that is left: a few of feet of rubble with a sprinkling of sand.

At least the sun is shining again and the sea is warm.

In other places, like Tulum south of Akumal, Wilma has actually made the beach several metres wider. A complete survey of the coastline is going on to measure the changes.

Meanwhile in Mérida, all the bakeries are selling Pan de Muerto - sugared bread with a really jolly pattern of bones on top. The Day of the Dead - *el Dia de los Muertos* - is fast approaching. In Mayan - the origin of the tradition - this is called *Hanal Pixán* and the ceremonies are still alive although struggling against the American import of Halloween with its more frivolous fancy dresses and trick or treats. Actually, it should really be called Days of the Dead as the first day is for departed children and the second for adults: 1st and 2nd of November (All Saints and All Souls).

In European Catholic countries, these days can be grim with visits to chilly winter cemeteries to put chrysanthemums on graves. My mother was an au pair in Italy and she has always hated these flowers since as there they are called 'fiori dei morti' - flowers of the dead. Here in Mexico, the sun shines in November, it's nice and warm and the dead are remembered with affection and - yes - it's another occasion for a celebration.

In Mexico, people don't try to hush up death. In fact, sometimes it can go the other way. The tabloid papers relish putting pictures of road accident victims - preferably dead - on the front page. They're not short of them either, with so many people cycling without lights after dark - even on the toll road to Cancun - and the general craziness of driving around here. And lately there's been an escalation in wars between the drug cartels with daily assassinations of gang members - some in Cancun - and they are also pictured in gory detail. It's hard to pass the newsstands without flinching.

But in Mérida as ever things are much calmer. Over the road at the university, the students set up the traditional altars for departed loved ones so they can come back and enjoy their favourite food and treats. A double line of candles on the ground leads to each white-clothed table.

On this altar, there are very formal framed black and white pictures of the dead relatives taken in studios long ago. Mostly they must be the students' grandparents or, more likely - as people tend to have children pretty young here - great-grandparents.

Vases of marigolds and roses flank the photos with more candles and sometimes a statue or ornate picture of the Virgin Mary jostling with a large number of little bowls filled with traditional foods for the dead:

- Mucbilpollo - this is a very popular dish that you can even buy in *Walmart.* It's like a big spicy chicken, pork and tomato pie made using maize meal and wrapped in plantain leaves and - in rural areas - cooked in the ground.

- Sugared bread rolls.
- Yuccas bathed in honey.
- Xec: A mixture of peeled mandarins, oranges and jicamas (sweet turnip-like roots that can be eaten raw).
- Rich chocolate drink.
- Atole - a sugary cinnamon milkshake made from corn flour.
- Fresh drinking water.
- Liqueurs.
- Beer.
- Fags and cigars - even if these are what finished off the dear departed in the first place.

Some altars are generously set up for floating spirits who don't have any relatives to welcome them back, so they can still have a good time.

Once the dead have been and enjoyed the essence of the food and other offerings, rosaries or other recitations are said, sometimes accompanied by a harmonica. And after the following words everyone tucks in:

'Ayer los muertos tomaron la gracia y ahora los vivos nos comeremos la grasa.' ('Yesterday the dead entered into grace and now the living can eat the grub.' Well, something like that.)

What these altars don't have are any sugar skulls - probably considered naff and in-your-face. For these, markets are the best source. I decide to take a trip to Santiago market.

I am thinking I might set up a small altar back home for floating spirits as I'm not sure if any of our deceased relatives will be willing to cross the Atlantic for the sake of some sugar paste.

Inside Santiago's covered market, I steer clear of the meat section full of carcases hanging from metal hooks and the sound of cleavers on wood - and head for the two or three stalls that have small mounds of sugar skulls. These range from the size of a walnut to ones as big as my fist. Most of them are decorated with lines of coloured icing sugar to create a skull cap and with sequins in the eye sockets. Even more disconcertingly they have names printed on strips of paper and stuck across their foreheads - Lucia, Pedro, Juan, Maria.

And one stall has a whole range of other sugar items: cowled monks carrying a bible, lantern or candle - or a perfect miniature *Corona* beer bottle. I should think that last one is unorthodox. I buy it straight away.

There are also three inch sugar plates covered with sugary flautas or enchiladas in case you don't have time to cook a real mucbilpollo; wreaths of pastel flowers and - wait for it - sugar coffins with lids, decorated with flowers. You pull a string, the lid lifts and up sits a skeleton and all totally edible.

I buy a whole selection, set them up on the kitchen table and email Martin a picture, saying I am going to sit up tonight to see if anyone comes from the other side to enjoy the sugary treats.

He sends a reply:

'Are you sure you're not getting carried away there?'

Probably. But there are absolutely no ghostly visitations and I head for bed at 10 pm.

Afterwards, I'm not sure what to do with the sugary display - it looks much too sweet to actually eat - so I put it in the fridge. Every time I open the door, a whole crowd of sequined eyes stare at me accusingly.

Something that really is almost haunting in Mérida is the sense of having stepped back into the past - all the tiny workshops and individual shops - and the feeling that they might vanish at any moment to be replaced by dull shiny chain stores.

Maybe the old can survive. Every day on the way to Santa Ana market, I pass an upholsterer's. It is so small that the furniture they are working on spills out over the pavement and onto the road. This is also a good advertisement for future business. And they sure work fast - whole suites re-covered in a day, dining sets of eight chairs no problem: leave them with us overnight.

Just within a couple of blocks of our house, there are two workshops where they produce decorations for parties and entertainments: cartoon characters painted onto flat foam panels; a chandelier and light fitting repair shop and a large trade and retail outlet devoted entirely to cake decorating. Here you can buy miniature plastic palm trees, sugar fountains, cupids and babies in cradles (pink or blue) plus enormous bags of icing sugar and tubs of jam.

You can, if you want, go up to Gran Plaza and have a *Toni & Guy* type of haircut at fashionable salon kind of prices. If you don't mind a wet cut with no fancy stuff, (a blow dry is murder in this heat anyway), and can take along a picture of what you want, a very nice cut can be yours for three dollars just around the corner.

But in the roads a block or so north of the main square, there are boarded up shops that must once have been very fashionable places to go. Now, the traffic speeds past the elegant signs. One that has often caught my eye - in typical stylish lettering across the front of the tiled fifties building in Calle 62:

Margot Ham, Salon de Belleza.

Now the steps just lead up to a padlocked door.

So what happened to Margot Ham? I imagine her in the nineteen-sixties, walking down the street in the early morning to open up the salon for the day. Her hair is set in the Latino version of the beehive, with heavily kohled eyes and blue eye shadow - both still very popular here - and a geometric print shift dress.

Did she move to Cancun to set up a salon there in the late seventies? Did she move north to the Gran Plaza, when all the new money started going there? Or did she just retire and no one wanted to take over the business?

I like to think of her still dancing every Tuesday night in Santiago square, to the live big band, where the best dancers are in their sixties, seventies, even eighties, and can foxtrot, rumba and quick step the youngsters into extinction, well into the hot, hot night.

I hope she hasn't met a tragic end like the person who lived in a house just off Santa Ana square. One day I notice that a front door has been sealed over with official looking tapes. Candles and flowers in vases fill the narrow doorstep. I don't like to ask but it feels like something bad has happened in this house. With a shiver I move on quickly to the bustling market.

Martin is getting worried I am *doing too much shopping* as I have now hit the shops just south of the main square, which is still a thriving area packed full of interesting shopping opportunities that you just don't get in your regular suburban shopping centres back in the UK.

Take the shop devoted entirely to car interior refurbishment. Here you can get materials for your seats: leather, brocade, vinyl, you name it - plus rubber matting, trimmings and moulded plastic.

I buy a thick rubber offcut as I am hoping to do something about a pair of sandals with toe thongs that are killing me as they slope downwards from a high sole at the back. Why not make wedges for the front, to even them out? No problem for anyone who was brought up on the *Blue Peter* children's TV programme. Well it does work. Except I get a few funny looks as it is really difficult to cut two inch thick rubber evenly.

If the B & B is still on hold, I can at least make myself useful. I start working a shift at the Mérida English Library. In keeping with the rest of town, this is quite an eccentric place, in the nicest possible way.

Firstly, it is in an old house: a colonial bequeathed by one of the founding mothers. It has traditional pasta tile patterned floors - designed to look like rugs and carpets - high ceilings and elegant doorways. The back room is open to a long courtyard where members and visitors can sit and read. The only drawback is the totally vicious black and white striped mosquitoes that obviously love books and invade the library, especially after rain.

So you can be browsing very happily in the crime section and then realise there are at least five killer mozzies up your skirt.

Back in the mists of time, I was a graduate trainee librarian in a university library and spent long peaceful afternoons putting barcodes into books in Medieval Archaeology and Old Icelandic in preparation for the first generation computerised system. You had to make sure that you put the twin barcode onto the right catalogue card or the whole library would be completely screwed up. They must be onto something like the twentieth generation by now.

Here in MEL, there is still a card system for lending books. And a card system like no other. First you need to know everyone's surname. And with Spanish names, that generally means the middle - father's name - as the last one is your mother's family name. Then you have to know when their books are due back. But the date in the book can be weeks out if they've renewed by phone. So unless you get really lucky, you end up going through the entire drawer of cards. But no sweat, the customers will wander off and look at more books while you get your act together.

And the library committee has decided that books are a higher priority than a computerised circulation system for a library that has no source of income except donations, subscriptions and fund raisers.

At this time, the whole outfit is presided over by a retired north American educator with a habit of suddenly bursting into slightly risqué songs about female adventurers. And one thing makes her really annoyed:

'No, we do not have books in Spanish, damn it. This is an *English* library to encourage people to read *English* books.'

As a volunteer, you are supposed to check the day book for messages. One example:

'Volunteers: call for help if someone walks in and says they want to join and then tries to borrow the newest guide on the Yucatán. We will never see either of them again.'

And a despairing note from a long-term volunteer:

'Does anyone know their alphabet or am I just sad?'

The library also has a great children's section and a story hour on a Saturday morning. One day, one of the regulars, who lives around the corner, comes back just before closing to remove a chocolate from the special 'secret' tin in the children's room because: 'My mom is desperate for chocolate'. There is nothing in the day book to suggest how to deal with this.

Most of the members get the hell out of Mérida after Easter so MEL becomes a very quiet place with only the fans thwacking through the long hot days. At least the annual exodus generates massive donations of books and if the library already has a copy, they are sold off at a bargain dollar each.

In addition, you get some very interesting visitors. One day, a middle aged Yucatecan man in a doctor's white coat rushes in about five minutes before closing.

'Can you help me with my English homework? Please, it's an emergency.'

Another morning, a beautifully mannered elderly gent in a formal suit comes and sits down at the desk. He opens a bag and takes out several CDs of songs in paper sleeves and a book of poetry. He has written and performed them all himself. It is really sad to tell him we can't buy any copies. He would do better to go to Santa Lucia square on a Thursday evening when there is a free show - always packed out - of poetry, singing and music; and stalls sell rather scratchy recordings of the famous performers of the traditional trova love songs from the twenties and thirties.

People are always coming to the door to sell things. Door-to-door salesmanship here is a true art and very hard to resist sometimes. Including the guy hauling round standard lamps entirely covered in plaited raffia. He plonks them down on the pavement like a mini forest and just waits while I admire them.

I give him a note of our address and tell him to call there.

'What the hell are we going to do with this?' demands Martin when I get back after my shift.

'It's a nice lamp and it's all wired and everything. It's a great feature!'

It goes into a corner, which I guess is what a standard lamp is designed for.

The lamp seller is doing the rounds on foot, like the ladies who go up and down the streets with a big pot full of tamales or other savoury snacks, knocking on the windows, calling out the day's special, their mournful cry echoing off the pavements.

One up from this are the vendors on tricycles. Now we are used to the megaphone blast from the ice cream vendor and can almost understand the message:

'Come on Señora housewife you can't afford to miss this at only two pesos and 50 centavos a scoop.'

The knife grinder has a long whistling note to announce his arrival. That is all he needs. Less is more. A series of poop-poops on an old rubber horn means the guy with a tray of pastries is doing his rounds mid-morning and mid-afternoon at just the moment when you might be having an attack of the munchies between meals.

Now just when I begin to think I've seen everything, I decide to go to the fair.

Yucatán state holds an annual three-week long fair every November at Xmatkuil, a few miles south of Mérida, where there is a permanent showground. It is like an agricultural show in the UK and then some, with horse riding displays; dolphin and shark shows; and pop bands, traditional music and discos into the early hours. Plus there are stalls selling products from all over the state and further afield.

Right; this will make Christmas shopping very easy.

Buses run every ten minutes from central Mérida - if you can find them. The newspapers publish the road where they stop but I wander up and down until I hear a marshal shouting out: '¡Feria, Feria!' and jump aboard. Locals are taking advantage of an additional bus service so there are masses of unscheduled stops along the way.

We meander through a couple of villages and then turn into the showground car park, passing the rodeo ring on our way. I follow everyone on the bus until I realise they were all going through the exhibitors' turnstiles to start work manning the stalls. The *paying* public have to go around the corner.

Once inside, things seem a little slow. It is eleven in the morning and most visitors are school parties waiting patiently in line to see the children's show inside a pink model of a castle.

I wander around some of the exhibition tents thinking I will be hard-pressed to find enough to keep me here for an hour. The state oil company, *Pemex*, has a model of one of its complexes out in the Gulf. During the last few months, the workers must have spent more time evacuating from hurricanes than anything else. In fact, some of the few hurricane fatalities were in a helicopter crash in the Gulf. And there is nothing about the current dispute at the petrol stations: *Pemex* is trying to install regulators at all the pumps to put an end to rumours that they can be fiddled to deliver a less than full litre.

I mooch on past the car tents, remembering the food hall at our local agricultural show where there are always a number of free eats on offer. No such luck here because it would take business from the tremendous number of snack stalls that fill the air with an overpowering smell of hot, overused fat. Here you can stoke up with sausage-shaped, grooved Mexican doughnuts called churros and deep fried plantains. Or try the polystyrene platters of chips with salchichas and lime wedges, being careful to avoid the ones-I-made-earlier when business was slow.

In one of the state-sponsored tents, I try some honey - the only free sample anywhere - and pick up a leaflet encouraging more people to go in for apiculture as a small business. Maybe that is what we should do? There is room in the garden for quite a few hives. Somehow, it might conflict with the B & B side of things. What if a guest gets too close and is enveloped in a crowd of angry bees? Now, if we'd bought that place with an orchard out in the middle of nowhere…

I move on passed the round tank and spectator galleries for dolphin shows, and another one further on for shark displays. What the sharks will actually do during their show is not clear. I don't think I will want to be in the front row. Unless I hang around for another four hours, I won't find out anyway as I've just missed a performance.

The one thing I really want to see is an exhibition of the famous mummies from Guanajuato in central Mexico. They've had a tremendous build up in the local paper and on TV. First hearing about them, we'd imagined they were ancient, like the mummies in Egypt, possibly from Mayan tombs. But no, the Mayans hadn't gone in for mummification.

These mummies are rather more recent; just too close for comfort. Due to climatic conditions in Guanajuato, nineteenth century corpses sealed in crypts there turned leathery and were permanently preserved by accident. If their relatives couldn't cough up the grave tax, the remains were ruthlessly removed and put on exhibition.

I buy a ticket and file into the especially climate-controlled exhibition hall. In the entrance lobby, there is an enormous, truly eerie, blown-up photo of a hundred-odd mummies standing in a crowd. Maybe it is supposed to portray the last judgement, with all the mummies come back to life? Religious music plays over the tannoy and there are various ornate flower arrangements suggestive of a funeral parlour.

So I enter the main exhibition with some trepidation. Inside, there are about seven mummies lying down in glass covered coffin-like boxes.

It reminds me of the old story book pictures of Snow White lying in a glass case, but here something has gone drastically wrong. All the adults look like they are screaming; their faces are contorted in agony. There are stories that some were interred prematurely during a cholera epidemic, their catalepsy mistaken for death, and came to inside the tomb.

And their bodies have shrunk to leather-covered skeletons with only shreds of clothing left. Their hair - including their pubic hair - is intact although they have little to cover their modesty, apart from boots, also leather, that have survived. Only one has a name card, and that is almost faded away.

I am thinking: if ever there was an argument for cremation, this is it. Who would want such a grotesque and public after-life?

Only a baby, lying in a satin-lined miniature coffin surrounded by preserved flowers, looks serene.

A few schoolchildren come rushing through the hall and out again, as if they are on a dare. Somehow that seems healthier than the quasi-religious atmosphere the authorities are trying to invoke.

Feeling ashamed, and with a shiver not just due to the fierce a/c in there, I rejoin the cheerful throngs that are building up outside.

A huge area is devoted to mechanical rides - helter-skelters, dodgems, haunted houses, roundabouts and try-your-luck-stalls with the kind of stuffed toy prizes you see the world over. There aren't many takers yet even though each attraction is playing incredibly loud pumping music in an attempt to outdo its neighbours.

I suddenly realise I've been going in circles around the fairground for nearly an hour. My head is reeling from this full-scale assault on the senses - all the boom-boom tunes playing out of sync with each other, waves of hot frying fat from the food stalls, garish twirling decorations on the rides, ninety-six degrees heat and flashbacks of leathery contorted bodies.

I find a spot in the shade and sit down. I need somewhere calm and peaceful. This is a Mexican fair, what did I expect? And I haven't even finished the special exhibitions, let alone started on my Christmas shopping. I down a bottle of coke and press on.

The exhibition of 'the most venomous snakes in the world' is at least in a nice cool tent. And they should be worth the extra couple of dollars for a ticket. Unfortunately, not. They are so comfortable in their glass boxes, with carefully recreated environments, that they are all fast asleep.

I begin to suspect they are plastic replicas until I spot the shed skins lying like ghostly twins in several of the cases. No doubt they are saving their energies for the regular interactive shows and photo opportunities. I decide to pass on those. At least I now know that boa constrictors aren't poisonous, they just squeeze you instead. Not sure how they got in there, then.

Suspiciously close to the snake tent, there is a large exhibition devoted to chickens including an enclosure full of squeaking chicks. Children are picking ones out to take home. I suspect that the new pet will end up on the dinner table before too long, or, failing selection, will be reluctantly double-billing with the reptiles next door at feeding time even sooner.

And now it is time to shop. For people who live in rural villages, a fair gives them a chance of buying household items at good prices. Mothers have taken lifts on the school coaches in order to get here. Otherwise, some can't afford the trip. They are making the most of it, digging through the mountains of t-shirts and skirts on the clothing stalls.

I check out all the plastic and crockery stands with an enormous and bewildering range of useful items, colourful accessories and downright tacky ornaments covering every bit of canvas, support pole and floor space. You must step incredibly carefully to avoid buying something 'by accident' as the signs warn.

What about a pail filled with a complete dining set for just a few dollars? Certainly they are handy to carry home, with the bonus of a bucket thrown in. Or moulded plastic fruit bowls in any colour of the rainbow for 50 cents each. How about filling them with dried fruits and chocolates for Christmas presents?

Very conveniently, there are several stalls close by piled high with richly coloured slabs of crystallised fruit: yellow flecked pineapple, dark red sweet potato, golden guava, rich green melon, terracotta papaya, dusky blue figs. The stallholder offers me a slice of this one to taste. And what about trying that one too? The sweet potato has a strong earthy taste and a dense texture; a far cry from the sugar encrusted fruit jellies in boxes back home.

Fantastic, all my Christmas shopping is sorted. But will I be allowed through customs in the UK with several pounds of sugary fruit? The Mexican customs won't even let a stray apple through. Well anyway, I buy several slabs to sample. After all, I have to know what I am giving people. I'm planning another trip with Martin when he gets back from the UK so we can re-stock then. I wander on, nibbling the pineapple that is tart and sweet at the same time.

Then my eye is caught by a stall devoted entirely to fridge magnets. There are miniatures of every kind of tropical fruit and veg; mini packets of wheat tortillas, cans of refried beans, *Sol* and *Corona* beer bottles; dolphins, sharks and butterflies.

I come away with a handful of realistic looking lizards. Well at least they won't poo behind the fridge. Then I see another stall and buy and buy. Excellent present idea: light to carry home to the UK and everyone has a fridge. I end up with a bag full of tiny plastic red and green chillies; little frying pans with real sardines glued inside; several turtles, hummingbirds and inch-high bottles of branded tequila (solid plastic, unfortunately).

Wait: isn't there some restriction on taking magnetic devices on board a plane? Will thirty fridge magnets turn themselves into a force to be reckoned with and cause massive disruption to the plane's navigation system? I wish I'd paid more attention in physics lessons: I haven't a clue. Better stop, then, in case this genius present idea also hit the dust. At least the fridge in Mérida will get a cheering up and the resident lizards may think they have rivals and stay clear.

Next stop is the art stall. Here you can pick up wooden framed prints for less than four dollars. Oil paintings have been reproduced on tough textured paper and the effect is really quite good. There are plenty of still lives. Full of vibrant exotic flowers in crazily painted vases, they look like the backgrounds in Frida Kahlo pictures. I buy two and am very tempted by the ornate pictures of the Virgin of Guadalupe that are full of little golden details, which make them look like Russian icon paintings. Then again, it might be sacrilegious to buy them just for decoration in such a devout country.

On the same stall, there are masses of wooden objects from massage wheels to toy trains; carved plates and boxes; brightly painted yellow drums and red hibiscus flowers for the Christmas tree. I buy some of those too. Well this beats the usual slog through the grim winter Christmas shopping crowds back home. But here it is hot, very hot. I just have to stop for refreshment.

The beer tents are doing a roaring trade. *Sol* is giving away chunky plastic beer mugs if you buy two bottles. I'm not much of a beer drinker myself which is really sad in Mexico but Martin will appreciate it. I join the queue. You pay at one point, get a voucher and then go to the bar area to collect your bottles and mug.

Ah, 'hay un problema.' Mexico actually has very tight controls on public drinking. So you are not allowed to take away unopened bottles: the bar attendants whip off the caps and fill up the plastic freebie mugs. How am I going to drink two bottles of beer? I will never make it home. I'll be staggering around the fairground in endless circles until I collapse. And I might get the wrong reaction if I just give them away.

The attendants probably think I'm drunk already.

'Excuse me,' I muddle my way through a very limited vocab: 'Please, I don't want these.'

'You just bought some beers and now you say you don't want them?'

'I don't want drink, now. Can I have with lids?'

'Not allowed. You have to drink them now, here.'

'But I don't want to drink now. For my husband.'

'What's the matter with her?'

'Don't know, where's her husband? Hope he shows up to take her away.'

'I want more vase instead.'

'You must buy two more beers if you want another mug.'

'In place of beer?'

'This is all very irregular.'

'Just give her another voucher instead of the beers, look at that queue.'

Gratefully I grab the voucher and head to the cashiers who stamp it and give it back. With some trepidation, I return to the bar and get my second mug.

Everyone in the queue looks on aghast. Is this woman crazy, or what? Who will give back two beers for a piece of plastic? Mad gringos.

I make myself scarce to eat an ice cream in the shade and watch the sheep and goats having showers to cool them down.

Four hours in, and I am beginning to flag. And there are still rows of stalls I haven't visited yet. How come when I arrived, I thought it would only take an hour to do the whole thing? And now it really is getting crowded with people in a happy finished-work-and-it's-Friday mood. There are long lines at all the food stalls - no more plates of chips wilting in the heat as they wait for customers.

Somehow, I really don't think I am going to make it to the evening shows. My feet are longing for the cool pool at home. Right: just one last effort and then I'll be on the bus.

Two more hours later, and I have finally finished my shopping after a buying frenzy at one of the many jewellery stands. We are not talking *Cartier* here but cheap and cheerful. So that's how all my female relatives end up with a charm bracelet for Christmas. They are really cute: one has all pink and silver sea life: shells; dolphins and starfish; another has little pairs of shoes - all mules as no one in their right mind wears anything else in this heat; another has a complete cowboy set: Stetson; boots; rope; jacket; stirrups.

And when they open them?

'It's quite kitsch, Mexico, isn't it?'

And there is one last thing, spotted just as I am leaving. Something I've always wanted since my sister came back with one from a student trip around Mexico years ago. No, not a handsome Mexican. Martin can relax. But he still might not like it: a highly realistic eyeball ring, complete with an eyebrow. Very Frieda. It is supposed to ward off the evil eye. If it manages this with hurricanes, I will be well pleased.

Chapter 14: Crunch time

Yup, decision time can't be postponed any longer. We have to open up the B & B now or we will never do it before our year off comes to an end. Originally we imagined it would be such a super success that we wouldn't need to go back. Now there are only four months left and we haven't even started.

I get on the bus over to Akumal to meet up with Martin on his return from the UK. It is the time of year Roberto most dreads: the owners' meeting. Almost all of us will be converging in one go. Red alert. But this year, we are all on our best behaviour. Everyone in Akumal is totally exhausted after two hurricanes and we are bloody grateful for all the work they've done. It has taken days and days just to clear the road so vehicles can get through to Half Moon Bay.

We all meet up at *La Lunita* restaurant - which occupies the ground floor - for our traditional owners' meal. Despite having a brand new refit completely trashed by Emily and then the whole place flooded in Wilma, *La Lunita* is operating as serenely as ever. Only the bedraggled palm trees in between the tables on the beach suggest the devastation since our last get together. The talk is all about how everyone is open for business again but the airlines haven't resumed many of the regular flights. A couple who also own a studio in Playa, usually a hive of up-beat activity, say it feels like a morgue:

'Everyone worked so hard to get back up and running after Wilma. And then nothing. The restaurants are open but they're twiddling their thumbs. Everyone is getting desperate.'

'People will be back for Thanksgiving.'

'Yeah, if the planes are running.'

'Fox is a miracle-worker if he can get Cancun beach back for

Christmas.'

'Well, I'm sorry to be selfish - if Cancun isn't up to speed, they can come down here instead.'

Everyone, everywhere along that coast depends so much on tourism, it is really scary. Before the start of the hurricane season it was one of the busiest years ever, partly because people didn't want to go to the Far East after the Tsunami. At least the hurricanes haven't brought that kind of tragedy here.

We want to say thank you to the staff. *La Lunita*'s chef is proposing to cook a cochinita pibil and we all chip in. A pit is dug for the pork to be cooked over several hours. But that morning, Roberto comes flying around the building. Guess what:

'There's an alert out. A tropical depression is heading our way and it's building to a storm. It could turn into another hurricane. You won't believe it, we may have to evacuate. We'll know in a few hours. We'd better stock up with some food in the meantime in case we can stay here while it goes over. Get ready to go into the bathrooms and stay there.' The bathrooms are the safest place to be as they are in the centre of the building and don't have any windows.

Roberto jumps on his motorbike to go to the mini super:

'I didn't have any time to get food in before Wilma, and I was so hungry. This time, I'll be ready.'

We all follow suit. It is cheese spread and crackers time again. One fellow owner is advising everyone to stuff their fridges with newspaper, to help things last when the electricity goes off. Unfortunately, we don't have any newspaper, only two ancient copies of the *Reader's Digest* left by guests long ago. Oh well. We sit and read the *Reader's Digests*, going to the window every so often to see if the wind is getting worse. The mood is glum. Surely we can't get hit three times in one season, can we?

After all that, it is third time lucky. The tropical storm dissipates after a few hours and everyone heaves a sigh of relief. Not least Roberto, who must have been wondering what it would be like to deal with a hurricane and all the owners in one go.

After the nitty-gritty of the four hour owners' meeting, held in our chairman's two-bed apartment, we are keen to get out and do some snorkelling. We head for Yal-Ku lagoon, ten minutes' walk away.

We've seen reports on the web that the lagoon is filled with brackish brown water. But that happens for a day or two after rain as the run off makes its way into the lagoon. And Wilma certainly brought rain.

About a year before, the lagoon had a 're-style'. Before this, it was completely natural with only wooden steps to get into the water and some stone benches to sit on. Then a huge number of statues also appeared. Some are nice rounded Mayan figures that fit in with the landscape. But others are fancy elongated statues of Pan with pipes and sea maidens, straight out of *Caesar's Palace* in Vegas. Not to everyone's taste.

We pay our entrance fee and wander along the narrow paths to the side of the lagoon. Hooray! The kitschiest statues have *gone.* Further investigation shows that Wilma has blown them into the lagoon and they are lying on the bottom, with the rainbow fish swimming in and out of them like a giant glitzy fish tank. Yes, we think they look much better there. Every cloud has a silver lining…

That evening, we sit down and have a serious discussion. Martin has been in the office while back home: terrible mistake, because he's now been roped back in to work as he is desperately needed. From now on, he is going to be working remotely almost full time. So money will be coming in again.

I still want to try the B & B, but we have to face facts. We will need to shell out on more furniture and furnishings and then we won't know how much business we will get.

'And Mérida is just too hot in the summer' says Martin, sitting on the balcony enjoying the sea breeze. 'So I can't honestly say I want to live there permanently, even if the B & B is a success and I can carry on working as a consultant.'

'We'll have to sell it, won't we?'

Visions of returning to freezing station platforms and long working days drag in front of me.

'I think so. Don't worry: I have another plan.'

'Ah,' I say, 'I think I know: over here instead.'

Yes by the sea where there is a cooling breeze that sometimes, in fact quite often if this year is anything to go by, turns into a hurricane. We are thinking of selling the property that has escaped any damage and contemplating buying more over here. Crazy or what?

Martin is right: we have to be realistic. We might love many things about Mérida - aside from the heat - but is it really the place for us long-term?

'We need to return to the UK next year to sort things out. It may be months or years before we've got a really workable plan in place that will let us live out here, at least some of the year. Mérida needs endless maintenance and it'll be hard to get a rental out of season. We should try and sell it before we leave. This coast is growing all the time and a couple of hurricanes aren't going to stop that. And we'll need somewhere to put the furniture.'

'You think we should buy somewhere just to put the furniture? We haven't got that much.'

'I'm sure over here is a better long-term investment. Plus it's easier and cheaper to get to from the UK. We should buy another place before it's too expensive. We won't be able to buy in Akumal now.'

We need to go further south. Martin has already been doing his homework.

'How about Tulum?'

Ah, Tulum.

'I thought beach lots in Tulum started at half a million dollars? Oh no wait a minute; you're not thinking of that ruined hotel, way along the beach, are you?'

'Well, why not?'

We once spent a few nights at a hotel on the beach in Tulum, south of the ruins. Tulum has always been pretty low key, partly because the electricity on the beach goes off at 10 pm. But that hasn't prevented some very up-market eco resorts from setting up and attracting celebrities to stay in their cabañas on the beach to get away from it all.

It has to be said, though, that some of these cabañas have plasma TVs and mood lighting in the hot showers. In between these exclusive little places, there are still the old hotels with cabañas that have huge gaps in the cane walls, just a hammock and a plastic chair for furniture, and shared cold salt-water showers.

A long way south down the beach, we had come across a building that had either never been finished or had taken a hit from a previous hurricane and been left unrepaired. Maybe it was too far south to make money. At that time, the road along by the beach quickly became a bumpy track once it had passed the first flush of hotels.

'Well I suppose it might be going cheap, after the hurricane.'

The beach front at Tulum has taken a bashing from the storm surge during Wilma's passage and bits of cabaña have blown all over the place. Not that you would notice with the wreck we have in mind.

'I've checked and I don't think it's for sale. Anyway, maybe that's being over-ambitious right now.'

'I don't know: it hasn't stopped us before, has it?'

But Martin is right. Enough of pipe dreams: we have to get real.

Much later, we find out that the ruined hotel was in fact the deserted seaside villa of the notorious drug lord Pablo EsCobár. And since he died, it's been bought up and turned into a hotel…missed our chance!

'We can try Tulum town instead.'

'That's a dump. Remember when we tried to find lunch there?'

Tulum town is about two kilometres inland from the beach, straddling Highway 307 as it makes its way down the coast. Back when we'd been staying on the beach, before we bought the flat in Akumal, we'd hired a Beetle for a day - yes, it was the only car available. That was number one mistake. It had terrible gears. Correction, it didn't have gears that any mechanic would recognise. Mistake number two was stopping in Tulum town on the way south to visit the ruins at Muyil.

We drove up and down, trying to find somewhere for lunch. There was not a good choice. In fact, there was no choice at all. And it was pouring with rain. Eventually we stopped outside a building that had 'Pizza' painted crudely across the wall.

The door was open: good sign. We went in. A few mismatched plastic chairs were leaning up against a battered table. I took a look inside a chiller cabinet: it was full of half-melted ice. There was no one around.

'I'm desperate for something to eat,' said Martin, pulling out a chair with as much noise as possible in the hope of attracting some attention.

'How desperate?'

Right then a lady in a pinny appeared from a doorway at the back and motioned us to sit down.

'Pizza?' We asked hopefully.

'Si', she said.

'Dos, por favour y dos cokes. Gracias'

'Si', she said and disappeared.

'What kind of pizza are we getting?' asked Martin, 'She didn't say'

'Edible, if we're lucky', I said.

But she was back again in a moment with some cold *Cokes* and straws and motioned that the pizzas would be following in due course.

We sat and waited for forty minutes.

The lady in the pinny came back in to tell us that they would be ready soon.

'¿Ensalda?'

'No gracias.' we chorused. That might delay things by another forty minutes.

Eventually the pizzas appeared.

'They're OK, just.' I said.

'Good thing we're hungry.'

We made our way through the pizzas while the rain tipped down outside, blowing a damp mist into the café.

'Hm,' said Martin as we sat in the car afterwards, 'don't think we'll be coming back here in a hurry.'

In the driving rain, we turned south and headed for Muyil, a site that was only just being excavated. Martin checked the petrol gauge.

'It's further than I thought. We'll need petrol soon. Look out for a station.'

It was hard to see anything through the streaming wet windscreen.

After another thirty minutes, we almost gave up. Martin pulled the car over.

'We can only go another five kilometres or we'll run out of petrol.'

'There has to be a station somewhere, with all these lorries coming up from Chetumal.'

'It's probably another hundred kilometres further south. We can't risk it.'

'Well let's just go on another five, and then turn back.'

Fortunately Muyil was just around the next corner. And it was well worth the effort even if it wasn't exactly Chichén Itzá. We had it all to ourselves. Signing the visitor's book at the entrance kiosk, we saw that on average there was one set of visitors every other day. The caretaker's family were living on site in a set of Mayan huts and their chickens roamed over the first pyramid that was still partly covered in small trees.

The caretaker's son, about five years old, offered to guide us. He led us along the overgrown paths between the ruins and then clambered up and announced from the top what it was: El Castillo or El Templo.

Last stop was a huge lake. This was within the protected Sian Kaan biosphere. A group of eco-tourists in a 4-by-4 pickup (very eco) were just embarking on a motor boat to do a tour. We could have gone along but it would last several hours. Martin was thinking Beetle and dark and no petrol.

We thanked and tipped our little guide and headed back to Tulum. At least the Beetle started and we managed to get back. What happened later is another story. Just to say that we swore never to hire a Beetle again.

'Right: Tulum town. Are you quite sure?'

To be honest, we have been through Tulum a few times recently on the bus to Mérida and it looks much smarter than on that rainy day a few years back. For starters, slip roads behind grassy borders have been added on either side of Highway 307 so that pedestrians and cyclists are protected from the through traffic. And there are more restaurants - in fact you could spend a fortnight here and not try all of them.

Plus now there are plenty of expensive looking gift and craft shops. The old backpackers hang out called *The Weary Traveler* might still be catering to the budget crowd but now there is money in town as well. All those boutique resorts on the coast are pulling in a new kind of clientele.

We decide to get a colectivo down there to check it out. Martin has seen a couple of possibilities on the web. No more ruined hotels: we are being sensible for a change. We are thinking now of somewhere we can stay when we come out and rent in between. No way are we going to sell up in Akumal but the overheads mean we can only stay there for a short time in between paying rentals. So we want somewhere with low outgoings.

A whole development of cube houses like those *Mr Kipling* French Fancy cakes is being put up along the Highway between the turn off to the ruins and the start of the town. They are being marketed to Europeans who want a little place in the Mexican sun and the starting price is around 70 thousand dollars.

The only problem is they haven't started building them yet. Martin has made enquiries and has been told there will be communal swimming pools and a bus to the beach, on site letting facilities etc. etc. Every time he asks: 'Will there be…' the developer's office say 'Oh yes'. That's worrying. Have they costed any of this? In fact, do they have the money to build the houses or are they waiting for deposits to come in?

Our colectivo passes the site: not much to see. Plus it is a long walk from the restaurants in the town proper, so not a brilliant rental proposition.

There is not a great deal else for sale in Tulum town, at least not publicly. We take a wander around the streets either side behind the fancy shops and restaurants lining the Highway. It is like Playa long before it got attitude: just a normal Mexican town with bumpy roads, dogs wandering around and people going about their business. It feels nice and relaxed.

In the main square there is a bandstand, a covered market and several football pitches. A strange long concrete building with a curved roof, dormer windows and open sides turns out to be the Catholic church. The sound of singing drifts across the square, mingling with shouts from the intensely fought football games.

We come across plenty of local eateries as an alternative to the tourist-priced fancy places on the Highway. And even there, we find several very reasonably-priced taco bars and loncherias where the locals are eating. Plus a huge number of internet cafés, all full.

The big question is: where is everyone staying? They must be on the beach as there are not a huge number of places in town: *The Weary Traveler*, about three budget hotels and one boutique place hidden in a back street called *Hotel Latino*. We have guests checking into Akumal the following day, so we decide to try out the *Latino* as it is offering promotional low season tariffs, including free bikes.

Shortly after we get back to Akumal that afternoon, there is a knock on the door. Is Roberto warning everyone of another approaching storm? No, it is two of the staff bearing plates of cochinita pibil. Hey, isn't it supposed to be the other way around and we are treating them? Well apparently there is plenty for everyone. We say thank you very much. Cooking in the ground certainly adds a little something. You won't find nasty tough meat in these parts as long slow cooking, whether in a pit or on the stove, is the preferred method.

Next morning, we head off to Tulum, doing a little maths on the way. We will really need to sell our house in Mérida before buying something else. But we can scrape a deposit if we see a place we like. Because, of course, Mérida will sell really quickly, won't it?

We check into the *Hotel Latino*. It is a tiny place built on one long thin lot. The owners have obviously decided to make a virtue of necessity so it is minimalist with a big M - actually, that should probably be a very small m. The pool is just about big and deep enough for two people to sit in clutching their glasses.

Pebble-inlaid incredibly narrow spiral stairs lead to the first floor rooms. No wonder there is a sign saying: *Watch your step*. Someone obviously has a thing for pebbles as they also cover the shower floor.

'I think it's to massage your feet. And the light is supposed to flicker and change like that: it's called mood enhancement.'

'Rubbish,' says Martin, 'the bulb's going.'

'This is the kind of lawn I like.'

It consists of long narrow earth filled boxes with a single line of grass in each of them dotted around the wooden terrace to *suggest* a garden.

'It said free chocolates on arrival.' says Martin, turning over the mound of pillows and cushions on the bed. At least they don't stint on the linen.

'I think it is just a suggestion.'

Now Martin has also seen something else on the web. This is a small development of about six houses around a pool, just south of Tulum town. The pictures look very nice. But they do say 'artist's impression'. Right, that means they haven't started building yet. In fact, it doesn't seem like anything is being built just yet in Tulum. Well that means we are getting in at the right time, doesn't it?

We head off to the real estate office that is handling the sales. The American guy who is running it invites us to hop in his jeep and he will take us right there. And incidentally, he is expecting the lawyer and some French clients that morning as they are putting a deposit down. We will have to move quickly to secure one.

He drives south on the Highway. About half a kilometre out of town, we turn off down a bumpy track with jungle on both sides and eventually emerge into a clearing.

We get out, expecting to carry on by foot.

'Great isn't it?'

Er: what exactly? Then we realise that there is a small party of workmen busy in one corner hacking at the scrub. There aren't even any foundations in place. This is it.

'Here will be the pool and those two have already been reserved. The one on the corner is still available. It doesn't have a direct view of the pool but that's how it goes: the early bird gets the best worm.'

He sees our faces.

'It's still a really nice house, that one.'

Well actually it isn't the lack of a pool view we are worried about. It is the complete lack of anything. This place makes that plot we visited in the wilds outside Mérida look like a veritable palace.

'When are you going to start building? The particulars said it was underway four months ago.'

'Blame Wilma. All the workers got pulled onto the reconstruction. These guys have only just been freed up. But they're making good progress. Remember that you're paying pre-construction prices here. Once they're built, the prices will go up like a rocket. Look, the developer's coming into the office this afternoon. You can ask him any questions you like.'

We get back in the jeep and he takes us over the Highway to the beach side of the road and pulls up at the end of a track that peters out after about fifty yards. Back in the office, we'd noticed a big plan of this area south of

Tulum, covered in little squares.

'There will be a new road to the beach. Believe me, these lots are selling like hotcakes.'

We'd read somewhere that this area was originally ejido land, which is communally owned by the local people and can't be sold unless they all agree and get compensation. The agent says this has been sorted, but then there will still have to be planning permission and infrastructure.

'How do you get to the lots?'

'Oh you take a trek through the jungle. One day, they'll be on the road to the beach. The front line has already gone.'

Returning to town, we take a diversion through the backstreets. He indicates a new building with a palapa roof and a 'Se vende' sign strung across the front, facing the market on the main square.

'Now that you don't want to see: it's a box. Mexican architects: they like little rooms. We're building real huge open plan living. The rentals will be great. Come back at four and ask any questions you like.'

Well there is no harm in asking questions, although we are not totally convinced. We have a happy afternoon on the beach where the sea, for once - it can get quite rough here - is absolutely still. We paddle in the shallows and spot rays undulating along right by our feet and, swimming further out, Martin sees a fish he swears is five feet long.

'What, a shark?'

'Could be'

'I think I prefer the pool back at the hotel, even if you can only swim half a stroke.'

Four o'clock and we are back in the real estate office, slightly beach-tousled and trailing fine sand.

The developer, another American, is a genial guy.

'Just ask me any questions you want. Hit me with them.'

'How many developments have you had here?'

'This is the first one but I've done plenty back in the States. We're building to US quality here.'

'When are you going to start building proper?'

'Well we got the deposits for the first block so we're starting on that.'

'What about electricity? We didn't see any poles. And water?'

'They're heading south out of town. We're kind of hoping someone will pay for them to reach this far before we need them.'

Right.

'What are the sewage arrangements?'

He looks startled. Well he did ask us to hit him with them.

'We'll fix that later.'

This guy is a genius: he's sorted the whole Mexican plumbing problem in one go by a simple solution: Ignore it.

We say thank you and we'll have to think about it.

Well we might be missing a fabulous opportunity here. On the other hand…and anyway, they want a 50% deposit as payment and we just don't have it. And the total price is more than we want to pay: 140 thousand US dollars. Tulum is not looking very hopeful.

'I know,' suggests Martin, 'Let's phone Hugo in Akumal and see if he has anything. He's bound to have some local contacts.'

Yes, Hugo does. In fact, he has two very interesting properties. He will be right down to show us around in the morning.

That night, there is a very loud evangelical rock band playing in the town square. They might be making music for the faithful, but the whole town gets a look in too.

'What did we say about Tulum being a sleepy little place?'

We meet up with Hugo, who is desperately trying to find a car wash. He's been all the way - fifty kilometres - down the beach road to the fishing village of Punta Allen at the end and his car is caked in dust.

'It doesn't look good for clients.'

'We don't mind, Hugo', we assure him. We've ridden down to the beach on the hotel bikes for an early morning swim and are looking a tad scruffy. He is probably thinking more of the American high rollers who come in to buy beach villas for several hundred thousand dollars a piece.

Luckily, there is a car wash just around the corner from the first property. Car wash in Mexico does not mean water jets. It means a whole family armed with buckets and chamois and giving your car a really personal touch.

While Hugo is checking his car in, we notice a pretty pink three storey building across the street with a 'Se vende' sign on it. Like bees to the honey pot as ever, we cross over to take a closer look.

Martin sighs. 'I think it's one I saw on the web. You won't believe it but it's a B & B. About six rooms or mini apartments, I think. Hold on though; the price is way out of our reach. Close to three hundred, something like that.

Rats, rats.

Hugo comes over to join us.

'I can make enquiries if you like.'

'Thanks, better not.' We are determined to restrain ourselves.

While the car is being attended to, we visit the first property.

'It's a double lot, which is quite rare', explains Hugo. 'And it already has six foot walls all around. That costs plenty to build. It's got all this going for it.'

It is being used as a weekend retreat by a hotel owner from Cancun who wants to free up some money to develop one here in the town. Everyone seems to be having the same idea.

The lot is in a block on the fringe of the town, across the Highway from the sea. It is off an unmade road with wilderness beyond.

'Should be quiet here,' says Martin, thinking of the racket the previous night.

A young man who is acting as caretaker comes to open the gate - accompanied by a Rottweiler. This is worrying: Tulum doesn't seem that kind of place. And inside, there is not exactly much to guard. In one corner, there is a shallow swimming pool, beautifully clean and inviting. The caretaker proudly shows us the mosaic terrace that surrounds it and hands us a card: he is an artist and this is his work.

The pool is the most substantial structure here. In another corner is a large but rather bedraggled palapa-covered hut. Inside, it has a kitchen, shower room, living room and a kind of hayloft above with a mattress in it. An outdoor shower, a well and a storeroom complete the buildings. The rest is tropical garden.

'There's room for two four bedroom houses here,' Hugo suggests. 'You can let them out and stay in one when you are here. It will be a really good investment.'

It certainly has a very nice tranquil feel about it. But where can we store our furniture? It looks like the hut will leak with the first hint of rain. Or are we just being over-cautious? Fortune favours the brave and all that.

We head on to the next property. Hugo drives towards the main square.

'This is a very good rental investment, although you probably don't want to live here yourselves as it's noisy. Very noisy.'

Ha! We draw up outside the 'Mexican box' that the agent yesterday had dismissed out of hand. What is it about this one? We are intrigued to see it.

The square seems particularly sleepy in the late morning sun. Horses are grazing on a huge empty lot next to the new building. But we know the stage for last night's band is just down the road. Maybe that kind of show only happens once in a while?

'It's three new apartments. There's hardly anywhere to rent in Tulum town and you can get a good income from tourists and people living here longer term. And the developer will do a deal if you buy the whole block. Maybe two hundred and eighty…Once you sell your house in Mérida, you can buy it.'

Phew, we are trying to be restrained for once but somehow we seem to have got the reputation for splurging out on property - I wonder why?

The builders are still finishing off the interiors. We look at the front: there are large pits ready to take the septic tanks. One tick at least. We have to walk a plank across the hole to get to the external staircase.

'The top one is best', advises Hugo, 'You can have a private solarium on the roof'.

We reach a large open balcony and go in. There is a wide living room with a bar to a kitchen, a cloakroom, three bedrooms and two shower rooms. We finish up in an external utility area. It is wrong to call it a box: all three bedrooms are larger than anything in a new build back home. And there are two or three windows in every room so it is very light. So maybe that isn't so good when the hurricane season arrives but that can be sorted with shutters.

Hugo points upwards.

'They can put in a staircase here to get to the roof. That will give another big outside space.'

Well, it seems like good value and it is in budget. Plus it is very central for everything in the town, including all the entertainment: maybe that is the problem.

'How often do they have musical events here?' we ask.

'Quite often.'

Somehow, we feel Hugo is telling us something here. But it seems like the only place for sale in town that will be ready to take our furniture and we can lock up and leave when we go back to the UK.

We all retreat to have a drink in one of the cafés on the Highway.

'Tulum is going to grow just like that in the next few years.'

We agree: we've already seen the changes since our last visit. Isn't this what had put us off Playa? Or have we gone all commercial now? Well being realistic, Tulum looks like a good investment. There is more talk of a new airport to service this part of the coast and the area way south that is now being called the 'Costa Maya'. But isn't Tulum a nice town as it is? Do we want to be part of a huge change that might spoil it?

We tell Hugo we need to have a think. It is time to get back to Mérida in case the pool has turned green with algae making hay in our absence.

On the bus back, we review the situation. It doesn't take long.

'We don't have much choice, do we? That flat is the only thing that's actually built already.'

'Maybe we're getting too hung up on our furniture. After all, it's only worth a couple of thousand dollars - seems ridiculous to rush into buying a property worth fifty times that just because of a bed and a fridge.'

On the other hand - what if we did buy the whole block? We could let out two and live in the other one and manage it all ourselves. Wouldn't that be an ideal solution? Once Mérida sells, we'll have just about enough to do that.

Except we haven't even put the Mérida house on the market yet: are we getting carried away or what?

So our next step is to call in the real estate agents again. It will be sad to say goodbye to the house, especially the garden and the pool. This is likely to be the first and last time we ever have our own swimming pool, but we've enjoyed it for a great year so we can't exactly complain. It really is time to face facts: we don't have a workable model for living here yet. And it is hot, very hot. We are already missing the sea breezes within minutes of getting off the bus.

The agent who sold it to us just a year ago comes around that afternoon. Right: she will take some pictures and it will be on the website tonight. Well: why put it off? We might as well get going straight away, now we've made the decision to sell.

She has good news on the valuation: it is more than we paid and should mean a small profit after deducting the money we've spent on it and agents' fees.

'We'll have plenty of viewings, I'm sure.'

We rush around tidying everything up, all excited, imagining a stampede of eager house buyers. Then I remember something Lucia once said:

'The people who buy in Centro are mostly Americans and Canadians who are retiring. It's also attracting gay couples as they feel Mérida is OK for them compared with other parts of Mexico. What they all want is an old colonial with original features, single storey, three beds and a courtyard with room for a small, easily maintained pool.'

Right, let's see what we have: Two stories, with two separate staircases. A modern interior. Six bedrooms and a huge pool that needs attention every day.

'Let's hope there are more crazy people like us out there', says Martin.

While Martin gets down to checking his work emails, I head to the *Chedraui* supermarket on the Paseo Montejo, where I'd seen some colourful Mexican fabrics. I've decided our interior needs cheering up: I am on the hunt for material that can be turned into wall hangings. Well, back in the UK, framed wall paper is all the rage in interior decoration isn't it? This is more or less the same thing…

Bingo: I find some cheap and cheerful woven wool cloth in bright green with little lines of yellow and blue cowboys, horses and cacti marching across it. Great: this will add some colour. Maybe it isn't exactly in the most restrained good taste, but this is Mexico not Kensington or Manhattan.

They always say you should have fresh flowers elegantly arranged around the place when selling. Well in this climate fresh cut flowers tend to wilt before they're even in the vase. No, sad to say it, but artificial flowers are the thing here for good reason. With Martin occupied up in the study, I head down to Centro.

'Just don't get carried away. You're maximum budget is five dollars.'

'OK'.

Just south of the main square, there are shops devoted to artificial flower arrangement with everything you can possibly need. It's not just the flowers you can buy, but all the vases, baskets, rinky-dink metalwork containers in the shape of bicycles and chairs, ribbons, feathers, garlands of plastic bougainvillaea - and, of course, the Mexican equivalent of garden gnomes: frogs. These are just the thing to add life to your indoor courtyard. There are frogs wearing sombreros, frogs fishing, frogs lying in hammocks: in fact they are much more versatile then gnomes and boy are they popular, vying with the Virgin of Guadalupe for prime position in many a front porch. But maybe this will be too Mexican for potential buyers?

There are some great arum lilies although they are too much per piece for my budget so instead I opt to get flowers that look like the ones in the prints I bought at the fair with huge orange and yellow petals. I confess I go cutesy myself and buy one spray complete with a butterfly on a stalk. I still have change left to buy a blue and white vase I've seen at the giant plastic and china emporium next door.

Right, that's the interior decoration done. All we need are some keen buyers.

Our house is now on the web:

'Blue and gold hacienda style in Centro.' Sounds good. The Mérida agents really can talk the talk. They'd probably curl up and die in shame if they produced the usual UK blurb: 'Six bedrooms, large garden and convenient for local shops.'

Well, the really hot house-buying time starts when people came down for Christmas, although our agent assures us that the season is all year round. I guess everyone always thinks the first people to see their house will buy it. We are no different. People like the exterior; the look of a hacienda, but inside it is 'too American'. They are coming here to get away from that.

We try lurking around when viewings are due to drop a few cautionary tales into the conversation. If they say:

'There's so much concrete. We want the old high ceilings with wooden beams.'

We reply:

'That's the great thing about this house. We know some people who spent a fortune doing up an old colonial and next thing they knew, there was sawdust all over the living room. They had termites *everywhere.*'

It doesn't even register. We try another tack, conjuring up visions of a colonial-style makeover.

'Of course, if we were staying, we would put in a balcony wrapping around the house so every bedroom could access the garden directly.'

They go to the big floor to ceiling sliding windows in our study upstairs and pull them open onto thin air.

'I don't like that.'

Why are people so picky? Why don't they fall in love with our house? All the drain problems have been fixed. There are no horrible smells.

One problem is that there are so many new agencies springing up in Mérida that buyers may never get to hear about our house. But the longer established agencies share buyers anyway if they don't have anything suitable on their books. As we find out. One of my fellow volunteers at the library, recommends the guy who escorts the house tours. He runs an agency: why not bring him on board? I approach him one day while everyone is gathering at MEL for the introductory talk before setting off on the tour.

'Oh, I know your house on Reforma. I've brought several people round already.'

Whoops.

'Nice garden.'

But it's a nice house as well. Honest.

Now in the house-selling world you should never jump to conclusions. Like thinking that someone who makes an offer over the internet, sight unseen, has got a screw lose and is just having a laugh. One day we get a call from our agent:

'We've had an offer in by email from Miami. The guy says the Mayan gods are telling him to buy your house. If you accept the offer, he'll send a friend down from Guadalajara to look at it.'

Why on earth did we turn it down?

Ok, the offer is some way below the asking price.

And the buyer has to sell property in Florida. And the Mayan gods might change their minds.

Why didn't we just say: yes, OK, come on down?

Afterwards, we kick ourselves.

Then one day, a rather picky pair of Americans have just left when we hear a commotion from the other side of the gate. Are they remonstrating with the agent for showing them a non-colonial? What is going on?

We peek out of the door in some trepidation. The agent is having a lively conversation with a slightly tubby Mexican guy wearing the standard afternoon siesta gear here: loose t-shirt and shorts. The two buyers are looking uncomfortable, if not down right scared.

The agent hustles them into the 4-by-4 and they drive off quickly. Next, the tubby guy approaches us. We are really worried: is he laying claim to our house via a long-lost will or some similar showstopper?

He introduces himself in very good English. His family are selling the old colonial next door, which is still for sale after several months. He lives across the street and noticed the buyers arriving and saw them go into our house. He thought they had made a mistake - after all, our house is just a house, isn't it? Not the kind of thing Americanos are looking for. But his house has it all: the floors, the beams, the courtyard, the grandeur.

Unfortunately this DIY approach seems to have scared them off altogether for all of us. Not that they had shown much interest in our house. Their viewing had taken all of three minutes. But if they had their eyes on an old wreck, they might have been able to do a good deal direct…No wonder the agent sped off. Our neighbour retires to continue his siesta.

'What happens if he tries to waylay all our buyers?'

'I know: they looked like they thought they were about to be kidnapped or something.'

'Well, I suppose someone might come along who wants to buy both and turn them into a boutique hotel.'

'Huh, that will be ironic.'

The other problem is timing. In the sleepy afternoon, the whole area is deserted. But if buyers came along in the morning or evening, it is all go at the university with students' cars treble parked in the wide curve outside our house.

We survey the mini parking lot outside:

'How come they can all afford cars?' Martin is indignant. 'We never could when we were students.'

Not only that, the cars are so tightly parked that alarms go off all the time. And the owner is inevitably stuck in a lecture for the next hour.

Early on, Lucia had marked out the space immediately outside our gates as a no-parking zone. The students' idea of what constitutes a through-passage won't let a motorised tricycle squeeze by, let alone a car. As we don't have a car, it is slightly - academic. But it won't look too good if the agents have to park in another street.

So we try to make sure it is 'inconvenient' for viewings in the morning. Sundays - fine, they can come anytime they want.

It just somehow happened to be the summer vacation when we viewed.

We are not alone in having difficulty selling. Very close to Centro, just south of Santiago square, we've passed a brand new highly angular modernist house. It is also for sale. With huge windows, a cool pool and designer finish, it is inexplicably languishing on the market.

'Maybe it's a red light district around here at night? Seems fine in the day.'

No, it is more like the problem is: it is modern. And you can look in the big, big windows from the pavement.

In another, very tranquil street next to a really well known boutique hotel, there is a great blue curvy deco house - with all the fittings intact. In the UK, this would be like gold dust. But here - no, it's not colonial.

Mérida seems to be giving the lie to that familiar mantra: 'Location, location, location.' Here it is: 'Features, features, features. And don't even bother if it ain't colonial'

'Looks like we will end up doing B & B after all,' sighs Martin. It is already December and Christmas is looming. We had hoped to have a sale lined up before we went back to the UK for the holiday. There will not be much time left afterwards.

Then Lucia comes up with an interesting proposition: why not swap houses with her Mom, Marisol? They would really like a big garden with a pool and their house can be more easily locked up and left - and it is right in Centro.

We arrange to go down there immediately. As ever, you can't tell anything from the rather dusty street just one and a half blocks off the main square.

'Hm: no parking', says Martin: the houses are all straight down onto the pavement.

'Well we don't need it anyway.'

Marisol invites us in, and immediately the noise and dust of the street have gone. Her house is a thirties deco take on the old colonial model. It still has the high ceilings and rooms opening one into the other and patterned floor tiles. But the doors and woodwork have clean deco lines.

We go out through the open living room into a courtyard.

'It's nice.'

'There are two more courtyards,' announces Lucia.

Straddling the first courtyard, there is a roomy stand-alone dining room with deco coloured glass windows all around. In fact, it is a thirties version of the now ever-so-fashionable orangery. It is filled with a deco dining set, sideboard and a massive armoire that takes up the whole of one wall. 'Hay un problema:'

'We are worried our furniture won't fit into your house.'

So are we. In fact, it is quite obvious it won't.

Lucia explains that the furniture came from their previous family house; an eight bedroom rambling casona on the Avenida Colon. This is a wide boulevard that runs west from the top of Montejo and is full of fantastic old mansions, some of them now offices, some very smart homes and others sadly neglected.

We continue on into another paved and gravelled courtyard with an avocado tree in the centre surrounded by a raised border to keep in the moisture. This is a classic Méridano garden. It is certainly a great deal easier to maintain than our crazy lawn.

'We have parrots here every morning,' Marisol tells us. And it really does feel very tranquil although you can see the only high rise buildings in town: the *TelMex* building and a brash condo-hotel called *El Castellano.*

Then we go through a gate into an even bigger courtyard with mango and orange trees. No need to go to the market for fruit here. And there is plenty of room to put a pool or even build an annexe.

'Wow!'

But the family furniture is a showstopper. And anyway, haven't we decided to leave Mérida? Somewhere in the back of our minds there is always the question: won't we kick ourselves in a few years' time when the centre of Mérida may be pedestrianised and has earned World Heritage status and it is *the* place to live? After all, don't the Guccis have a place here somewhere already? How long before the beautiful people pour money into rescuing all the dilapidated palaces?

'I don't care - it will still be too hot', points out Martin. 'Let's get back to our original plan.'

And then Martin is called out on an urgent mission to Japan. He is flying back to the UK from Cancun so we both decide to go over via Tulum to have another look at the apartment. Martin reminds me of another cautionary tale we'd heard about Playa.

'Remember that story about the guy a few years' back who thought he was paying over the odds for a run-down corner building on Fifth Avenue? Fifty thousand US. Just five years later and it is worth ten, twenty times that?'

'I know: Tulum could go the same way. That's when we'll get out. And I bet that's why the locals are not selling yet. Why shouldn't they hold on and cash in on a boom?'

We get off the bus at Tulum, cross over the Highway and go to have another look at the outside of the apartment building. It is very peaceful in the early evening. The market is not exactly the most dynamic of places and the shops around it seem to open at the whim of their owners. There is a florist selling headily-scented fresh flowers and a piñata shop next to it, with a whole galaxy of Christmas stars hanging from the ceiling.

'I like Tulum: it feels nice.'

'Yes, I can imagine living here.'

'Those pizzas we had on the Highway last time were the best I've eaten outside Italy.'

That does it then.

We go straight ahead and put in an offer on the apartment, to include construction of a solarium on the roof. Martin has one day back in the UK to organise transferring the deposit before heading out to Tokyo.

A week later, I am back over from Mérida to sign a preliminary contract. Hugo takes me along to their 'back office' in a secret location where his colleague counts out ten thousand US dollars for the deposit which will have to be taken to the Notary's in Playa. He hands me the money in a brown paper envelope for safekeeping.

I try to act nonchalant, clutching it tightly. What if I drop it on the street in Playa, filling the air with clouds of hundred dollar bills? I'm very glad to reach the safety of the Notary's office.

A solicitor, rather than the Notary, is looking after this initial transaction. The developer turns up with two colleagues for moral support and advice. It seems this is his first venture on this coast as he actually lives in Mérida. We all cram into the solicitor's office.

Four hour's later…the contract has been signed. It isn't that there is a big argument just that we go through every line and plenty of changes are made. Basically, once we have paid our next instalment - up to half the purchase price - we will be able to take possession. Great, we can move our furniture in pretty soon after Christmas. The final payment will be made once a condominium regime is in place for the building, allowing a separate title for each apartment.

Before we all leave, the developer renews his suggestion that we can get a very good deal if we buy the whole building. A little light comes on - maybe he will take our house in Mérida in exchange? Now: that *will* be a great deal.

'Where is your house?'

Ah: Centro. Now if it had been a nice new modern house up north in *La Ceiba* by the golf club and riding school…

Right: obviously a non-runner.

That night, I have a dream we've bought so many houses we can't remember where they all are. So maybe Madonna and co. can afford to run households all over the world. But what on earth are we doing?

Chapter 15: Buen Navidad

Once upon a time, we'd had great plans that everyone would come out to stay with us for Christmas. Now there seems to be a massive reluctance among friends and family to do this. Hey guys: what's the problem? Do you really like the UK in December when it's damp and grey? There never is a white Christmas these days, so why hold out for it?

Maybe we have carried on too much about how bloody hot it is. But December is actually the nicest time of year. In fact, it sometimes gets down to sixty in the evenings and is almost chilly. At the start of December, I even have to go on a mission to Centro to buy some blankets. And the shops are full of woolly jumpers.

The thing is that houses here in the Yucatán don't have any kind of heating. And even in parts of the country where it routinely gets quite cold in mid-winter, many houses don't have any. In more northern, higher parts of Mexico, they have to issue public information on how to keep warm.

The other thing is that maybe people will miss their traditional Christmas dinner if they come out here. But there will be other things to try: in the markets and even in *Walmart*, you can buy sides of dried cod. We examine it dubiously: it looks like salty yellowed cardboard.

'I'll pass on that', decides Martin. 'It's fish and it smells horrible.'

'It's very traditional.'

'Do you really want to cook it?'

The answer is no. Perhaps we could be tempted by another speciality? *Chedraui* supermarkets have whole leaflets full of special Christmas dishes to order, the choicest being roast suckling pig complete with stuffing and an apple in its mouth. There are glorious full colour pictures so you can see exactly what you are getting. Turkey does not seem to feature very largely for Christmas. Well, people eat it most days shredded in various dishes so it is not exactly a treat.

The local bakery is now selling the closest thing to fruit cake we have come across here - usually the best you can find is Madeira slabs with a few raisins scattered about. This is dark like ginger cake crossed with Dundee, with fresh grapes on top and it comes at something of a premium.

Somehow, the crystallised fruit I bought at the fair has all gone. But now all the shops are selling the rich coloured slabs along with dates arranged in great swirling platters. Most of the year, raisins and prunes are the only things widely available.

Down in the street of piñata shops in Centro, all the papier mâché pumpkins and witches from Halloween had been replaced by Santas, Christmas trees and brightly coloured stars with long gold streamers attached to each point. I buy a small one, about five inches across, for two dollars.

In a road just off the main square, there is a shop devoted to miniatures. Here you can pick up all those little scenes in boxes of skeletons doing everyday things: going to the dentist, the disco, playing volleyball on the beach. The shop also has stylised papier mâché trees of life with Adam and Eve at the foot and various birds and animals - including the serpent, of course - hanging out in the branches.

Now they have coloured tin Christmas decorations for the tree: bells and candles, Santas and stars - and poinsettia flowers: *the* Christmas plant here. I buy a few to feel more festive.

As we are going home to the UK, we aren't buying a tree. Just as well as there is fierce competition to get the best fresh Christmas trees especially imported. In fact, most people seem to buy theirs in early December. You are lucky to find anything later on.

In the evening, people are leaving their front doors open so passers-by can admire their tree. From the street, you can catch glimpses of a modest front room filled by an enormous tree draped in ribbons, decorations and lights.

In some front courtyards, there are huge, almost life-size cribs set up around the statue of the Virgin of Guadalupe. Over the road on the grass in front of the university building, there is an enormous all-in-one inflatable nativity scene - with Santa figuring largely in the adoring crowd around the manger.

In another front garden just up Reforma, we stand and admire giant plastic snowmen along with a crib, Santa and reindeer with sparkling antlers.

'Don't you think we're letting the side down, not having a life-size Santa climbing up the front of our house? And a Rudolph and sleigh on the roof with flashing lights?'

'No,' says Martin. 'There's enough in the neighbourhood already. Don't you dare.'

Right, we don't want to go for overkill here: just a few blocks away, an electricity pylon has been turned into a towering Christmas tree that sparkles alternately red, green and gold throughout the night.

Now the Boxing Day tradition of giving tips may be dying out in the UK, but here it is alive and well. One day before Christmas, there is a ring at the gate. Our postman is standing there with some envelopes in one hand and a printed card in the other that says:

'I am your postman and I have served you diligently all year round so now it's your chance to return the favour.' Well that is a big hint.

It is obvious that something is needed or - according to another of those urban myths that might well have something to it - we might never see any post again. Not that we have a great deal - mostly utility bills.

Pauline once tried an experiment for us, posting a letter from the UK. It arrived a month later, though according to a stamped date on it, it had languished somewhere in Mérida for at least a week. The previous owners had obviously not been generous enough. Or maybe they had been super generous - the post here is notoriously slow and businesses use couriers instead - and perhaps a month is pretty good going? I hand something over and hope it will be enough. At least I get our post for that day in exchange.

Over in Tulum, as we sit out eating pizza, a steady stream of carol singers comes by. These are groups of schoolchildren clutching torches and shoeboxes with home made cribs inside. They are also carrying something that looks like a cross between a crucifix and a Mayan tree of life, made from wire and covered in baking foil. Tulum is in the area where a sect who worshipped the Talking Cross (really a ventriloquist who inspired the locals to fight back against oppression) used to flourish and some of the practices are still carried on.

The group positions itself in front of a set of tables and starts half-singing, half chanting Christmas carols they've learned at school. We aren't sure, but these groups may be 'Las Posadas' - re-enactments of the wanderings of the Holy Family looking for shelter.

There is a pause after the carols and a tin is thrust forward. If you put something in, there's a final quick song thanking you for your generosity and the group move on.

Now in the UK, the holiday season is well and truly over when everyone trudges back to work after New Year. In Mexico, the festivities carry right on until February 2nd - Candlemas. On the way, there is el Dia de los Reyes - the day of the three kings on January 6th. Children put out wish lists the night before and hope for presents from the kings.

In the week before, all the bakeries everywhere clear their shelves so they can fill them with *Roscas de Reyes*: these are sweet bread rings topped with candied fruit and a cover of glacé icing. They come in a range of sizes: the biggest are about the size of a car tyre. There isn't any other bread available so I buy one.

'It'll just be that boring dry bread inside.' complains Martin.

But there's a surprise: I almost crack my teeth on something hard, and retrieve from my mouth - a plastic baby Jesus. In fact, there are two hidden in the bread. We check on the internet to see what this means. Right: We should really have been sharing the ring with a big gathering. Whoever finds a baby Jesus in their slice has to host a party for everyone else present before Candlemas. What happens if it is the host who finds the baby, is not clear. Maybe that's why there are two babies in the ring. Well, I hope it is only two.

And after Candlemas, there is absolutely no time to get the mid-winter blues because everyone throws themselves straight into preparations for Carnaval - the biggest party of the year.

In the meantime, I head back to the UK from one direction as Martin is flying in from Japan. We have a couple of days to get in the Christmas pudding and mince pies. Pauline joins us on Christmas Eve. Over the mulled wine, she pops the question we dread:

'So what exactly are your plans?'

We look at each other.

'Well, we are thinking we need to rationalise.'

'I would say.'

'I mean, we might set up a B & B over here and open it during the summer, when you can get the best occupancy. I'll run it and Martin will do consultancy. In the winter, we'll go out to Tulum for a couple of months.'

'Are you really sure you want to do B & B? It never got off the ground in Mérida, did it?'

Fair point.

'It's just that somehow it didn't seem the right thing to do in the end. Well, you know: it is too darn hot.'

'You got cold feet.'

'No, hot feet', corrects Martin.

'Also,' I continue, warming to my theme, 'if we try it out here first, there's the possibility we can still do it later in Mexico, once we've got the practical experience and our Spanish is better.'

'Looks like you might have to in Mérida, if you can't sell it. Run B & B there in the winter when it's not so hot, and come back here in the summer.'

Well, yes that does look like the likeliest scenario right now. In the meantime…we need to sell our house in the UK and find something that we can lock up and leave but that will also lend itself to B & B. And we want something that costs less than our current house: a very tall order.

'I'll go and look at properties for you,' offers Pauline, 'you know I love house-hunting.'

In fact, back in November, we had seen a property in north Devon that looked ideal: an old court house (very secure, obviously), complete with the original holding cells that would add novelty value to the B & B. Exactly what kind of clientele it would attract was another issue…

Pauline volunteered to check it out. But her report came back with a definite no-no:

'The cells are - well cells and feel like it: really tiny. And there is a smell of damp. You won't like it.'

So who are these crazy people who fall in love with properties over the internet?

After whizzing around seeing everyone and trying to sound like we know what we are doing, we decide to hold off any changes in the UK until we come back for good in March.

It is a couple of days after New Year. The pool and garden in Mérida have been left for nearly two weeks. Martin needs to stay to do some work. There is a cheap seat on a charter leaving the following morning.

'I volunteer to go back,' I say, looking out at the cold grey sky and pulling on another jumper. 'I'll pack right now.'

Chapter 16: Moving on

Back to Mérida in the middle of the night: somehow, it doesn't feel the same as that first time I arrived at the start of our great adventure. Reality is beginning to bite again, with a vengeance.

As I get out of the taxi, I can hear a horrendously loud rasping noise from behind the gate. I hurriedly pay the driver and, fumbling with the lock, tumble through into the dark courtyard.

The pump that pushes water up to the roof is on, and is straining and screeching away: it sounds like it is about to explode. I rush around trying to find the switch to turn it off and, a desperate half an hour later, finally trace it to a socket on the far wall. I just hope this racket hasn't been going all through the holiday.

I stumble out into the back garden, tripping over all the palm fronds that have come down in the last fortnight. Water is cascading off the roof. Something is obviously broken.

I turn off the water at the road and crash into bed. Happy New Year and happy new plumbing problems.

Señor K's guys are around again in the morning. Each section of piping on the roof has a small venting tube that sticks straight up. A big quince tree in the next door garden has blown around and knocked one of these off. Water started gushing out, emptying the tank, triggering the pump into over drive. I've got back just in time. Either the pump or the neighbours were about to go into orbit. But it just needs some solder and it is fixed. Phew.

Next I have to rush around and clear up, in case anyone comes around for a viewing. This is a prime time with people down for the holiday season. With damp all down the apartment walls left by the cascading water; it is just my luck if someone turns up this morning. I open up all the windows and doors to dry it off as quickly as possible. In this heat, it won't take too long, will it?

Even in the places that we saw on the house tour that had been lovingly restored, there was still damp seeping up the walls as the bedrock is so close to the surface and the concept of a damp proof course doesn't seem to exist here. So I can always say it is 'natural seepage' if the worst comes to the worst...

The pool is full of leaves, twigs and about thirty oranges bobbing around like a giant bowl of punch. It takes more than two hours hard labour to get it back into shape. Martin is right: a pool is great, but in the tropics it sure does need an awful lot of TLC. And we've been warned not to empty it because then the concrete will crack in the heat. So we are kind of stuck with it - however, if you live close to the beach, you can get swimming for free and with absolutely no maintenance. Yes: Tulum is a good move.

Once I've tidied up in Mérida, I need to head over to Tulum to take possession of the flat. We've wired the second payment and, although we still have half left to pay, we will be allowed to move in. That is, if it is finished. In new builds here, you rarely get any fixtures or fittings, let alone a kitchen. As part of the deal, we've paid for a kitchen and wardrobes to be fitted.

Apparently, American visitors get very hung up on closets. It makes more sense in this climate to have open hanging spaces but US renters want doors. They probably won't be able to sleep in a room without doors on the wardrobes. We've been told it is that serious.

I roll up a cushion from one of the sun loungers to use as bedding, get up at 5 am and head back down to the bus station to catch the early bus. In Tulum, I meet up with Hugo and the developer and we do a tour. I diligently tick off the items on the snagging checklist we prepared back in the UK.

Hooray - the stairs up to the solarium are in place. It is just that they are rather steep. In fact, they are more like a loft ladder. But once up on the roof, and with a new palapa in place to give shade, there are great views right across town. However, even in a slight breeze, the ends of the fronds are whipping about. The whole thing will be flying off at the first hint of a hurricane. Then again, we might be lucky next season - there may not be any hurricanes. Think positive. OK, I'll try.

In the kitchen, there is now the biggest stove I've ever seen. It has six hotplates and a big griddle on top, an oven and a broiler. There is also an incredibly thick and highly polished pale limestone surface in which you can actually see the fossils.

The developer, to give him his due, included some nice touches in the original spec - like basins created from slabs of the same limestone and huge fans in all the bedrooms, as well as the a/c. Judging by the jolly breeze blowing through the apartment, though, neither the fans nor the a/c will need much use.

However, there is still some finishing to be done on the famous closet doors. I am beginning to wish we hadn't bothered: they are all misaligned and the cheap raw wood has been painted in blotches. There's been some sort of problem with the carpenter and another has been brought in. No worry: he'll be back tomorrow to finish the job.

I am given the keys and we all shake hands.

'How is your sale in Mérida coming along?'

'Lots of interest.'

'No offers then?'

'Er,' - did that strange offer by email count? - 'not exactly, yet. But our agent is very optimistic.'

'You know, you could still have all three apartments. If you can put down half now, you can have the other two to use straight away.'

'Thanks: that's a great offer. I'll talk to Martin.'

Why don't we push the boat out and take a risk? Hold on: we need to try out living here first to see exactly how noisy it is. Remember what everyone has said? We don't want to be lumbered with a whole block of flats where our renters regularly decamp in the middle of the night because of the din.

That afternoon, I take the bus to Playa to buy a mini fridge on special offer at *Walmart*. A fridge is the one thing I really have to get. And a can of pesticide: I spotted a couple of cockroaches doing a recce of the apartment as we went around this morning. I wander through the huge store that is crowded with all the tourists renting condos in Playa. It is almost fisticuffs at the bakery counter, the queue is so long.

The taxi back practically wipes out the saving I've made. What on earth am I doing going all that way to Playa? I promise myself I will look for a store in Tulum for any more furniture purchases. After all, we should be patronising local businesses. And Playa really is more like a city now. It is nice to be back in the peace and quiet of Tulum.

I unroll my cushion and flop down exhausted. Nothing will keep me awake tonight. Well, there isn't any music at least. Now whoever said that country villages are tranquil places has never spent a night in one. Tulum really is still almost a village. And in villages, people keep animals. Horses: fine, they're pretty quiet. But in Mexico, almost everyone in the country keeps chickens. Tulum is no exception.

I am just nodding off, hoping I won't be too confused when I wake up and find myself lying on the floor in a strange place, when some firecrackers start popping away. Well, that is not so bad but any commotion and all the cockerels in town obviously think that they have a new rival on the scene. Right in the next lot, the loudest bird I've ever heard starts cockadoodle-doing like crazy. Then the rooster on another block decides to join in, and then the next one. The cry is taken up all over town.

I look at my watch: it as only eleven at night. I thought they were only supposed to sound off at dawn. Dawn. Uh-oh.

Sure enough, come first light, they are all back on duty.

'Come on, you're in the country now. It goes with the territory. You'll soon get used to it. Don't be such a wimp.'

Well I have to be up bright and early anyway as the carpenter is due at eight. Ten o'clock comes and goes. I pass the time watching the world go by. The apartment building has been built on a lot half way along the block. Maybe it has been sold off to raise money by the family who seem to own all the land around it. I feel literally like I am in an ivory tower, looking down on the sprawling collection of single storey huts and concrete buildings that surround our building.

Then I look closer. Right: now I can see the source of that regular chopping sound. So this is where all the chickens come from that end up in the two smoke houses on the Highway. Our neighbours are running a low-tech yet obviously highly efficient chicken preparation line. This is how it works:

- First step, select the chickens for that day from the coop.
- Next step, despatch them. This seemed to involve putting them head first into buckets followed by a quick coup-de-grace.
- Third step, pluck.
- Fourth step, grope inside and pull out the yucky bits.
- Last step, chop up.

Pity the noisy old cockerel is always going to escape the chop.

A smoky fire is burning constantly close by. I am trying to work out if this is just to get rid of the unwanted trimmings or for roasting, or both.

'I think I'll stick to cheese for the time being.'

Just then the carpenter and his mate turn up. And I can tell they are not in a good mood. They mutter something about the developer promising to come along later.

'And if he doesn't there'll be trouble.'

It isn't difficult to guess there is an issue over payment. Well, we've given the money to the developer so he can sort this one out. But this is strange: I thought he said he was heading back over to Mérida last night?

Anyway, they set to work with a will and I go out to get a good supply of chilled coke to try to keep them sweet. Then I head off to look around town to see if there are any furniture stores. We need a bed and a plastic table and chairs: yes, we are going for minimalism again, at least until we bring the furniture over from Mérida. Pity we didn't ask for hammock hooks to be added as that's one thing that surprisingly wasn't in the original spec.

First stop is the *San Francisco* supermarket about a kilometre up the road. They sometimes have plastic furniture if you're lucky. Today, there is only a big pile of red children's chairs and another one of ironing boards and long queues of tourists at the two open checkouts. So where is everyone staying? Well, there are many self-catering villas along the coast in places like Soliman and Tankah bays.

We'd even briefly considered buying a plot in Tankah Bay and took a hire car down the bumpy track to take a look. The plots were cheaper than other parts of the coast. Then we saw people heading out from shore in canoes, to avoid the thick weed. And our car was attacked by a pack of semi-wild dogs, leaping onto the bonnet. We couldn't speed away as they were right under the wheels, everywhere.

'This is terrible; we're going to be stuck here for hours.'

'You know, this is the day I've finally decided I don't like dogs.'

Eventually someone came out of one of the high-walled houses and called them off. Well, it might be a great place to stay but it sure didn't seem like it that day.

'What a friendly place - wouldn't like to take an evening stroll here.'

'I think we're agreed that's a no.'

'You bet!'

Now why hadn't I seen that yesterday - a great shop right on the Highway in the centre of town, full of furniture and fridges at reasonable prices. I order a bed without delay. It will be delivered tomorrow morning, for free. Well, it is literally just across the road. And do they have plastic chairs and tables? Not just at the moment - I should try a place a couple of blocks back. Excellent: I will go there later on. In the meantime, I'd better get back and see how things are going.

I climb the stairs and push open the door. There is a kind of snow all over the floor. It is nestling on top of a layer of a glue substance they've been using on the closet doors. Then the carpenters mate appears, pulling his feet up one after the other from the sticky floor.

He looks like he's aged forty years in two hours. His hair and eyebrows are white from the wood shavings he's been planing off the wardrobe doors. I offer him another coke, hoping he isn't about to choke on all the stuff he's inhaled. The carpenter emerges from the back room and indicates it will be about another four hours.

'The developer is supposed to be here at two to pay us.'

'Right,' I say, 'that's great.'

It seems like a good moment to get out of there again. I head into the back streets to find the plastic furniture shop. Tulum peters out about three blocks away from the Highway on either side. So it shouldn't be difficult to find the place.

I trudge up and down in the full sun. That shuttered building might be a store, when it is open. Then I think I've found it: a kind of mini-super cum bakery with a couple of plastic chairs outside. Great. I am just about to pick them up and take them in to pay when the owner and his wife come out and plonk themselves down in the chairs. Whoops. But they must have got their chairs from somewhere, mustn't they? And surely they hadn't gone all the way to Playa for them?

I search on. There are chairs outside all the little shops - for the owners. Sod it I'd had enough of this for one day; I don't mind sitting on the floor. I get something, though, before Martin arrives tomorrow evening.

I return about four and things are not looking good. The developer hasn't turned up.

Now unfortunately I know enough Spanish to recognise a big moan.

'We're not leaving until we get paid. He'd better hurry up and get here. We've done all this work and we bought the wood. He owes us two thousand pesos.'

I try to make sympathetic clucking sounds without getting too drawn into it. All the same, I can see I need to do something.

Right. I don't have the developer's number. I phone Hugo.

'Hugo please help. The carpenters aren't happy. They're expecting the developer to come and pay them.'

'He's in Mérida.'

'So he's not driving back this afternoon?'

'I shouldn't think so. Listen: I'll try to speak with him. Let me have a word with the carpenter.'

I hand my mobile over. The carpenter is really not happy. He goes on for fifteen minutes. Rats, that is all my credit gone.

Feeling fed up, I head over the road to buy a top-up card.

'I can't face going back in there just yet.'

So I go into an internet café and send Martin a cheery email.

'Going fine. All services working. Work nearly finished. See you tomorrow!'

Five thirty and the carpenters have finished the job. To give them credit, they've done the best they can and removed all the mess from the floor. I am feeling quite sorry for them.

Then I try turning on the kitchen tap. No water. All the taps are dry.

Just then the phone rings. It is Hugo. He's left a message for the developer and hoped to speak to him soon.

'When you do, can you tell him the water's gone off as well?'

'No problem.'

The carpenters leave their bags on the balcony and go over to the market to get a snack.

'We'll be back.'

I sit down and eat some chocolate, the first thing since breakfast. Who said new property is hassle free? Why didn't we go for that lot with the nice little hut on it?

Just then, Hugo rings.

'We have a solution.'

'That's great.'

'You pay them.'

'Right. Great idea.' How come I hadn't seen this one a mile off?

'And someone is coming around to fix the water. The carpenters will pay him out of the money you give them.'

'How much?'

'Don't worry, we'll take if off the final payment.'

I turn out all my money on the floor: just enough to pay. Right on cue, the carpenters return. I count out the cash. The atmosphere immediately improves. They indicate they will hang around for the agua.

The man to fix the agua turns out to be about six people - one to fix it, the others to act as assistants. Up comes the cover on the underground chamber that houses the water tank. Then there is some fiddling about with raw wires. The sparks flying make it look pretty damn scary.

Then hey presto, the pump is working again. To check it, one of the assistants starts watering the grass in front of the building. An oldish guy with a pot belly approaches me and lets me know he is just 'a poor campesino' who is an important element in the agua recovery operation. The tips seem to be clocking up here and I have hardly anything left, even in coins. Just then money changes hands between the carpenters and the chief water guy and everyone seems to be happy at last.

The only problem is I will have to explain to Martin how come I've blown two thousand pesos in one afternoon.

That night, I am in bed by eight o'clock. First, though, I very carefully shake the sheet to check for cockroaches, and spray a circle of pesticide around my makeshift bed hoping it won't do for me instead of the nasty little blighters. The wind is really whistling and groaning through the apartment tonight. I wish I had a blanket. In the end, I have to get up and put on the one jumper I have with me and a pair of socks, and use a towel as an extra cover.

'This is ridiculous: I'm in Mexico.'

Oh well, at least Martin won't suffer from the heat here. He is going to be very happy.

The bed arrives spot on time and the delivery guy won't even take a tip after hauling it up to the second floor. The only problem is that I only have one single sheet with me. And linen outlets in Tulum seem to be as rare as plastic chair shops. Rats: I have to go all the way back to Playa. By the time I realise this, it is lunchtime. Better get my skates on: Martin is due to arrive at five. Knowing my perennial luck, I will get stuck in Playa and will return to find him sitting on the steps outside, steam coming out of his ears. And not from the heat, for once.

Given I have just blown the entire furniture budget on paying twice for some dodgy closet doors, I am going to be very restrained in *Chedraui*, and only buy a set of sheets.

Three-thirty sees me running the ten blocks south to the bus terminal, clutching a bucket, a mop, two sets of special offer sheets, three towels, a quilted bed cover, a loo brush and holder - and a large gooey chocolate cake to celebrate our new home. Oh, and yes, I decided we need a futon so I've ordered that as well. And now it looks like I am going to get back very late.

The next bus - the local *Mayab* stopping service - is just about to leave. I buy one of the last tickets. However, that doesn't stop more people getting on after all the seats are taken. A very comfortably upholstered lady with a sleeping toddler sits down next to me. She also has a big bag of provisions, a large newspaper and a radio. The rack space is already taken.

I put my feet in the bucket, the mop ever so elegantly between my knees and pile everything else up to my chin. The driver shouts to everyone to hold tight: there are almost as many people standing as sitting, and we set off.

About ninety interesting minutes later, I extricate myself and my load of clobber and run across the road to the apartment. Martin is bound to be there. Why does this always happen? How come I am never organised in time?

Phew: no irate figure standing at the top of the stairs. Still, there is no time to lose: I have to make up the bed, make sure there weren't any cockroaches about and sweep down the steps that are covered in strips of palapa that have blown off the roof. I just hope this is like the trimmings that come out after a haircut, not full blown alopecia otherwise there won't be any palapa left in about a week.

'I've just got off a transatlantic flight,' remarks Martin, 'and I look fresher than you do.'

'Don't ask.'

'By the way, where do we sit down?'

'At the moment, there's only the bed. Or the floor. It's quite comfortable sitting on this lounger cushion. It's a really multi-functional piece of equipment.'

'Is that a cockroach I saw in the loo?'

Rats: I'd forgotten to check the cloakroom.

'We really do need to get a table and chairs. That can't be too difficult around here. There must be places that do plastic furniture. Look at all these cafés - where do they get their furniture from?'

I decide to change the subject. I am really so sick of plastic chairs.

'Well come on then: let's go out to a café so we can have a nice sit down.'

We go to one of the snack places on the Highway and order quesadillas - and chips for a treat. A tourist group wander by, see the bowl of chips and sit at the next table - and order chips all round. Then another group walks by and sits down, and another. One of the proprietors comes rushing out, jumps into a taxi and it screeches off into the night. Is he fed up with everyone ordering gringo chips? No: he is back in ten minutes clutching two large sacks of potatoes. They've never had a run like this before.

'Well it's three in the morning for me now, so I'm ready to go to bed,' announces Martin.

'I'm glad to say it's been really quiet these last two nights - that is apart from the cockerels. You get used to them.' I try to sound confident.

Nine-thirty at night and we are just settling down.

'This is really peaceful.'

'Wait a moment: what's that?'

'Sounds like a band tuning up.'

'It's too late for anything to be starting, isn't it?'

No, it isn't. The next moment, there is a terrific roll of drums and the band plunges into the first number. We can hear every word as clearly as if they were standing right by the bed. A rock concert at Wembley has nothing on this volume.

'They can't get any paying customers, can they? When it's so bloody loud you can hear it all over town.'

'Want to go over and see?'

'No I do not.'

The paying customers are certainly getting value for money. At two am Martin suddenly remembers he picked up some earplugs on the plane. He dashes out of bed, rummages around in his case and triumphantly produces them.

'You don't have a spare pair, do you?'

He can't hear me and anyway, he is already fast asleep.

Well, I am kind of enjoying the concert. All the numbers are very upbeat and rhythmic. I lie there, tapping my toes. There is not exactly any other option really. At three am, there is an announcement. After playing and dancing for five hours, they are finally calling it a night - or day, almost. Hold on: not so fast. A huge chanting starts up:

'¡Otra! Otra!'

'¡Otra! Otra!'

OK, they are calling for an encore. And they are going to get one. This is not just one measly number but a very generous forty-five minutes. They finish off with a Spanish version of Abba's Chiquitita, always very popular here. Phew, wind down at last.

At nearly four am, peace finally - well almost. There is laughter and chatting from the street as people stream away from the dance.

Next morning, I am feeling like I've danced the whole night too. Martin is more cheerful.

'I was fine after I put the earplugs in. Good thing I remembered them.'

'It's alright for some people.'

We head down the stairs on the way to the beach. Just outside the building, there is a large electricity pole. Plastered around its midriff is a big colourful poster for last night's 'Baile Espectacular.'

'How come you never saw that so you knew it was going to happen?'

'I had other things on my mind yesterday.'

In fact, after that we realise there are posters on practically every lamppost and pole in town. And just in case you miss those, there are advertisements six feet high professionally painted onto any spare wall going in town.

We'll have to keep an eye out in future, so we have some warning.'

'Or maybe we can actually go and join in?'

'We'll see. If we're renting out, there'll have to be a generous supply of earplugs on every bedside table.'

'I don't know - we can turn it into a plus: free concerts from the comfort of your own rooftop solarium.'

'Speaking of which, we will have to do something about that huge window.'

It certainly is scary - the incredibly steep steps down from the solarium head straight towards a six foot plane of glass before turning the corner. One stumble and you will be flying right through it.

'We'll have to put some bars across. I'm sure we can find something back in Mérida.'

The afternoon is spent cleaning and hunting for plastic furniture. We go up and down the back streets. It is a great way to get to know the town, not to find plastic chairs.

We admit defeat. They're probably down the one road we haven't checked and no doubt we'll find them next time - when we don't need them anymore.

On our ramble, we notice several new properties under construction, including what looks like a small hotel with a bar and café just along the road. Although building work is going on all around him, an immaculate barman in a white coat is optimistically preparing for an evening rush.

'In a couple of years' time this place is really going to change.'

'Well I just hope it doesn't become a city like Playa, because we'll be right in the middle of it.'

'Isn't that the idea?'

'I suppose so, but I like it how it is.'

'Look on the bright side: the more hotels there are around the central square, the more pressure there'll be to turn down the volume at those concerts.'

'Or not: what if this becomes bar central? They'll drown out the noise with their own hullabaloo like some of those roads in Playa.'

Anyway, it is time to get back to Mérida. The familiar pool anxiety is creeping up on us. Martin has never forgotten the time back in the summer when he got back and found the pool water had turned into a globby green soup.

This time, though, all is fine. But the next morning, Martin is looking a little pale at breakfast having been out first to do the pool.

'Hey, what's the matter - are you OK? Are you feeling faint? Quick: have some *Coke*.'

'There was something in the pool.'

'What?'

'Looked like a baby opossum. It was about a day old with a long snout and tail already. I'm afraid it was dead when I got there.'

This is the first time the pool has claimed a casualty - we've managed to rescue anything that has strayed in before, including lizards literally walking on the water, unable to climb up the slippery sides.

'I think the parent must have put its long snout down to the water to drink and it was clinging to them and fell off.'

'That is really sad.'

We try to distract ourselves by going out to find bars to fit across the dangerous window in Tulum. What about curtain rods and brackets? I volunteer to call in at the shop on the way home from the market. Their prices have gone up since we bought supplies when we first moved in.

'How much?'

'Just as well I didn't buy any then, isn't it?'

'Yes.'

'Anyway, I decided to go into *La Casa del Cheesecake* on the corner. I thought we should try them before we leave.'

Cheesecake is quite big in the Yucatán and is not an American import, as you might expect. I'd been put off by my previous encounter with the bread and butter/cheesecake combine from the bakers that dropped through the scales. However there is a nice aroma of freshly baked cake coming from *La Casa del Cheesecake* that operates out of a corner colonial painted sea-blue. Inside, there is a waiting area with seats and, reassuringly, a large chiller cabinet filled with shelves of baked cheesecakes.

You can choose from one slice up to a cake big enough for 40 people. And then you select the type:

Plain, strawberry, chocolate, amaretto, various other liqueurs.

I order a chocolate one, not quite knowing what I am going to get. The proprietor indicates for me to sit down and wait while it is prepared. As in many of the traditional shops, there are framed religious texts on the wall, a picture of the Virgin of Guadalupe, plus here a sign asking customers not to pass into the interior of the shop. Maybe people get carried away in anticipation of their delicious cake?

A few minutes later, he reappears with the cheesecake under a plastic dome. A plain base cake has been transformed with a chocolate topping, carefully piped in criss-cross lines.

'Do you think this is too rich?' I ask Martin when I get back.

'I shouldn't think so. Better try it now though, just in case.'

No problems.

We aren't doing too well though on the window bar front. There is nothing suitable in the hardware stores, even the gent in *Los Dos Camellos* has to admit defeat although he has come up with brackets for us.

'I suppose we'll have to try *Walmart.*' Martin hates that place with a vengeance. After a couple of minutes in the echoing interior, he will be pacing up and down like a caged animal.

And their hardware section has nothing suitable. We are passing the special offer row on the way out when Martin sees just the thing:

Brooms with rigid metal handles on special offer at two dollars each.

'These will be ideal.'

'I don't think you'd better dismantle it until we've bought it.'

'We need eight rods.'

'Do you think they'll let us buy eight? It might look suspicious like we're trade or something.'

'We'll have to do it in stages. First we take two each, and go to separate tills. Then we meet up outside.'

Martin gets through quicker than me.

'Ok, now I'll wait out here with the brooms and you go back and get two more loads. Make sure you go to different tills each time.'

'This is ridiculous. I feel like we're nicking them or something.'

'Well I'll have to stand here holding an armful of brooms, that's much more ridiculous. All the old ladies keep smiling at me. They must think I'm a great help in the house.'

The worst part is walking home carrying all the brooms. They aren't heavy enough to justify a taxi. We expect someone to stop us and buy one at any moment. Now we know what it is like to lug your wares around the baking streets.

Back at home, we set about dismantling the brooms.

'So what are we going to do with all these broom heads?'

'They'll be useful when the old one wears out. Also, you can have one for indoors and one for outside. And so on. Just change them as you need.'

'You always did watch too much on QVC shopping channel.'

We hurry back over to Tulum. I am en route to the UK, coming back in a couple of weeks with my parents who have decided they like Mexico, despite the dodgy plumbing and even dodgier grass.

After a couple of hours drilling and fitting, Martin stands back to admire his work.

'That's safer now.'

'And who cares if people say 'hey look at those bright yellow broom handles all over the window.' At least they can't sue us for that.'

Chapter 17: What a carnaval.

It's four am in the morning.

We all stagger up the steps to the apartment in Tulum. I fumble with the lock. Martin is probably fast asleep. Just our luck: we picked a charter flight that was delayed eleven hours, and had a jolly day at Gatwick airport, enjoying breakfast, lunch and tea there. We began to feel like the Tom Hanks character that gets stuck in an airport for months. And then there was the ten and a half hour flight and a ninety minute taxi journey.

I suspect my parents are deciding they don't like Mexico after all, although they are acting very game. Martin has got everything ready and we drop into bed. Just before I nod off, Martin whispers that it is lucky in some ways we didn't arrive earlier: he's already had a broken night after finding an enormous spider, bigger than his hand, crawling over the bedcover just as he was about to get in.

Somehow, he managed to trap it in a bowl and throw it outside. Then he'd gone around blocking up the various holes around the apartment - he is sure it had crawled up one of the empty TV cabling ducts. After that, he still couldn't sleep too well.

'I kept on thinking something was crawling over my face. Remember that time I woke up coughing and thought I'd swallowed a spider? Imagine what this would be like…'

We have to be up bright and early as we were off to Mérida to catch the big Carnaval procession next day. Well there is little chance of a lie-in anyway with Señor Rooster next door.

We all troop off feeling slightly jaded to a small bakery in the backstreets that has a café attached. The fresh juice and coffee with crumbly pastries go a long way to restore us all. In fact, we feel so much better we decide that there is time to hit the beach before catching the bus. Martin has already bought our tickets, as they always sell out fast even with three services a day to Mérida.

As ever in Tulum, a taxi materialises the moment we start looking for one.

'Where do you want to go?'

'To paradise, please!'

El Paraíso beach bar and restaurant operates out of a great circular open palapa and once featured in a beer advertisement. Remember those cinema ads showing a beautiful beach: 'Peckham on a rainy night when you're drinking Bacardi'? Hmm, it is quite like that. The beautiful beach part of it, that is. Except that it is a tiny bit blowy today.

My parents head off along the beach for a stroll and paddle in the water, as they adjust to the heat after wintry Britain. Then we see them coming back after just a couple of minutes. Mexico really is not working out this time.

It is so windy, the sand is blowing straight into their eyes. I really shouldn't have boasted about that ad.

Then we have to rush back, grab our cases - hoping the spider has not sneaked a ride - and jump on the bus. As usual, it stops at Valladolid and some of the tourists as well as locals disembark. What are we missing? Valladolid is a pleasant sleepy colonial town but it doesn't seem to have any special claim to fame. One day we too will have to get off and stay here, just to find out.

Back in Mérida, Carnaval activities have been going on all week. Tomorrow's parade will be the grand finale. A whole range of Carnaval kings and queens, princes and princess have been chosen. Martin chanced upon a burlesque show in Santiago square where the king and queen looked like London's pearly kings and queens and about the same seniority. However despite their grey hair, they were dancing on stage with people dressed up as giant rabbits.

'I don't think I quite got it,' says Martin, 'but it was entertaining anyway.'

There are also kings and queens chosen from 'people less capacitated' and schools. So everyone is in with a chance to shine, sparkle and shimmer.

The big parade heads into town from the top of the Paseo Montejo, moving down Calle 60 and into the main square before finishing in a park. Calle 60 is quite a narrow street at the best of times. Crammed with spectators, it will be incredibly claustrophobic and amazingly hot.

So we head for the wider, leafy Paseo, in the hope there will still be some room left. With two hours to go, we are just in time. The spectator seating on the central reservation has already been taken. Everyone there has that settled in, satisfied look of people who have got up monstrously early - and it has paid off.

'Maybe we should have slept out here,' suggests Martin.

The rest of us groan.

The normally sedate pavement is a swarming jumble of food stalls, sound stages, chairs, tables, awnings, drink coolers and open grills. The front gardens of the Paseo mansions had been fenced off and are being jealously watched by the security guards, who don't mind being on duty today.

'We really could do with something to sit on.'

No sooner have we said the word, than a vendor comes by with armfuls of folding wooden seats. They are yours for keeps for just five dollars. Or the deluxe model with arms is seven dollars. These are the fastest sellers on the street. You need to be quick to get them. We grab.

'Thanks: we'll have two of these and two of those.'

Now we just need somewhere to put them.

'Quick, over there, behind those tables. The people are all sitting down so we'll still be able to see.'

Even though it is four rows back, it is a good position. We set up camp, tucked in behind two tables. Just to our left, there is a private awning with a large family party in full swing. The mama of the family is busy piling people's plates high with goodies from a long line of plastic containers spread along a table at the back.

Spiced potato salad? Albondigas (Meatballs)? Fishcakes? Empanadas? Stew? Salad? Rice? Spaghetti? And, of course, tortillas and salsa. And not forgetting the beer. And nuts and crisps and pork scratchings. Then what about a little custard flan or bread pudding or some polvorone almond biscuits?

My mother starts calling her 'the great provider.'

And it is only ten in the morning. We try to work out if they are having desayuno (breakfast), or merienda (second mid-morning breakfast) or comida (lunch) or a mixture of all three. Or perhaps it is just a snack. Whatever, the party will be completely stuffed by the time the parade starts. Good: they will be too full to stand up and block our view.

Mind you, how come we've brought absolutely nothing in the way of refreshments with us? It is getting quite tantalising watching all that food. We are almost tempted to reach out and help ourselves. I rush to the nearest snack stall to get some soft drinks and crisps.

The crowd is thickening all around us. People were now standing four deep behind our chairs, with various babies and toddlers resting on the seat backs.

One keeps trying to poke Martin in the ear with a tin whistle so we suggest that he (the toddler, not Martin), should sit on the table in front of us, which means he can concentrate on blowing the whistle instead. Bad move.

'Don't even think about needing the loo,' advises my mother, which of course triggers just those thoughts. These kinds of events really don't take into account people with weak bladders. We've seen a whole row of portaloos in a side street but it will be impossible to reach them for the next few hours. At least it is so hot the liquid is coming out other ways.

The spectators in the stands over in the middle start making Mexican waves and a great blast of cheering and clapping comes from far up the road. At long last - the parade must be starting. The sound stages - manned by various radio stations - leap into life, pumping out the latest hits - *Gasolina* obviously featuring strongly.

'Just as well we decided not to sit by that stage back there,' says my father. 'It's loud enough here a hundred yards away.'

We can hear roars of approval from further up the road. Everyone in front of us stands up. Hey guys come on: you've got chairs. We don't dare stand up in case the people behind press forward and we can't sit down again. Then everyone sits down anyway because they've been premature. Maybe that's how the Mexican wave was invented. Another fifteen minutes pass before the parade finally reaches us.

First come the children's groups each on foot and followed by a float with a fantastical scene peopled by huge papier mâché unicorns or mermaids, serpents or devils. There are supposed to be three themes to the procession: Fantasy, magic and mystery.

'What's the difference?' I ask.

'It's obvious,' says Martin, snapping away with his camera.

Attendants in track suits dart in and out of each group, handing out water bottles here and tweaking a wilting costume there.

Every so often, everything comes to a complete halt and the float lorries blast out a set tune. The groups, already a little tired, flash automatic smiles and twirl and dance through a routine, keeping their heads straight under the huge headdresses. Everything turns into a blur of gold and gauze, streamers and ribbons.

However, Mérida is Mérida, not Rio. Under their scanty costumes, the women and girls are wearing flesh-coloured body stockings so as not to be too revealing. Although in some cases, this just emphasises the bulges. Cased in nylon, no wonder they need the water bottles.

Many of the costumes are on the same design - a huge headdress rather like a velvet spider sprouting from the head, reaching almost to the ground, held together with gold or silver voile or turned into two primary coloured wings. One group, to be different, has crinolines that are so large that their skirts are supported on wheels.

And now here come the centaurs. After all the frou-frou, they are really restful on the eye. In fact, they are very good on the eye: men with bared chests and horns sprouting out of their heads and tight hairy trousers. They have a whole extra body and hind legs, all resting on little trolleys that sway along giving a quite realistic movement.

'That's the fantasy one,' says Martin.

We are getting the impression that the biggest draw for some spectators is the commercial floats. No, actually it is not the scantily clad beauties on the *Sol* and *Corona* lorries. It's what they are lobbing into the crowd. Yes, Carnaval is the biggest freebie fest of the year.

The crowd rises, not to applaud the participants but to be in pole position for the free gifts whizzing through the air. How galling after all those months of preparation, sewing and practising to be outdone by a free packet of crisps.

'Well, better get into the spirit,' says my mother. 'Quick, catch that one Martin.'

'Got it.'

'What is it?'

'A packet of paper napkins. I thought it was something more interesting - everyone is making such a fuss.'

'It's very useful.'

'Another here,' announces my father triumphantly holding up a plastic *Coca-Cola* beaker emblazoned with this year's Carnaval themes and logo.

Then I snatch a paper eyeshade.

'How come we can't get anything edible?'

'Because that family in the tent are grabbing it all.'

'They can't still be hungry!'

The passing parade is beginning to turn into a blur. My father and Martin risk standing on their stools, wobbling around as they try to get better shots.

As ever, the people who get the best views are the ones sitting at home in the cool, watching it all on the telly.

'But it's the atmosphere,' says my father.

'Yes,' says my mother, 'including having soggy tortilla poked down one's back by toddlers who have had enough.'

After two hours, the last float straggles by, the participants looking somewhat despondent knowing that, by the time they reach anywhere, people have seen it all already.

Then suddenly everyone is on the move. We try going south to the nearest side road. A wall of people is surging the other way. So we head north with the crowd.

Up by *Walmart*, a huge sound stage is just gearing up for an evening pop concert. Boy, does this town have stamina.

'I think we'll pass on that.'

Once off the Paseo, the crowd thins.

Martin takes in a deep breath.

'I can start breathing normally again now.'

We trudge along, lugging our wooden stools, looking for a taxi; they've suddenly all disappeared. Eventually we get one to take us the last half mile - it is worth it, just for that.

That evening, with no food in the house and all the shops closed for the holiday, Martin and I set out in search of a pizza place called *SaZ'Zip*. They keep putting flyers through our letter box with a rather cute cartoon showing a delivery boy on a skateboard. The last ad made much of the fact that they opened on holidays. It is about our only hope unless we head into Centro and everyone is too tired for that.

We walk a couple of blocks north and east through the sleepy residential streets, doors and windows open to get any breeze. In one big old house we pass, you can see right through and it obviously had a makeover in the sixties. There are big metal chairs suspended from the ceiling and chunky coloured furniture surrounded by Afghan rugs.

People sitting by their open doors nod amiably.

'Wait a moment, we must have passed it. I bet it's closed.'

We retrace our steps.

Well this is supposed to be it. The two ladies we just passed sitting by the door nod agreeably again.

'¿Pizza?'

'Si.'

We try hard to place our order with them until they call a young man from inside the house. Then we understand. They are actually customers waiting for their pizzas, even though they look like they are really at home and settled in. Maybe there is quite a long wait.

The young guy motions us in to a cavernous front room sparsely furnished with a battered dining table and a large old telly. He gives us the latest version of their flyer -which seems to serve as the menu as well - because the special offers have been updated.

Do we want home delivery?

No, probably safer to wait as the motorcycle delivery drivers have difficulty spotting our house and we are so ravenous tonight, we really don't want our dinner going west again, literally.

We sit down at the dining table. Apparently you can eat in here if you want to. It does not look like many people ever take up the offer. Those memories of a desperate wet lunchtime in Tulum come flooding back to haunt us. However here they are taking on the big boys *Pizza Hut* and *Dominos* at their own game by offering all the trimmings - except they are doing it in the inimitable nonchalant Méridano way.

The kitchen must be way out the back as there is no aroma of cooking. This is place is so low-key it is really almost cool. *Pizza Express*: you are trying too hard.

We are really getting into the complete car mayhem in the movie showing on the TV, when the guy reappears with two pizza boxes. He shows us they also contain the garlic bread that came with the package and hands over a bottle of coke as well. We return home in triumph. Why do you only ever find these places when you are just about to move away?

A day later and my parents are off on the bus to Chichén Itzá. We are going to meet up again later back over on the Caribbean coast. Before they head off, my mother asks, kind of casually:

'So Martin are you really going back to work in three weeks' time?'

Whoops, somehow we've been so busy with other things it has crept up on us. Martin's face falls a mile.

'That means we need to get back to the UK next week. So there's time to get readjusted.'

No way are we going to sell the house and have everything done and dusted before leaving. Once my parents are on the bus, we have to move fast.

First, we need to move house - in three days flat.

'We'd better get the furniture over to Tulum now. Then we can let the apartment out. That's more likely than letting this house. There'll be less to worry about here as well if it's empty.'

Quick: call Lucia. She can help us on two scores: finding a reliable removal firm and she also offers to caretake for us in exchange for use of an apartment, pool and garden. Not a bad deal really, though we suspect the grind of looking after the pool hasn't hit yet.

The removal guy calls around later that day. It is going to cost marginally less than the value of our furniture.

'OK, we'll go for it.'

That evening, we start packing.

'How come we've got so much junk in just eleven months?'

'Don't look at me.'

'I'm volunteering to go over to Tulum to be there when they arrive', announces Martin.

'What about the rest of the packing?'

'I'll be out of your way so you can storm on with it.'

The removers - father and son - arrive at seven in the morning and make quick work of it. By nine thirty they are off, saying it will take about eight hours as they will have to go carefully over the speed bumps in every village and then there are all the potholes on the road into Tulum. So why didn't we think insurance was necessary?

I have a quick final confab with Lucia, promise we'll be back soon, and jump on the bus once more. So who said we'd given up commuting?

Somehow, in the rush, I've forgotten this might be the last time we see the house so I don't say a goodbye. Maybe that's the right way to do it. And you never know. I am still hoping we might be back next winter.

There isn't any time to dwell on it. Mid-afternoon and I am back in Tulum. Martin is hard at work sweeping and getting ready. We sit on the floor and share a bottle of *Coke*.

'What do we do if the van never turns up?'

'I'm sure it will. It just might be quite late tonight, that's all.'

But at five, there is a toot from down in the road.

'Wait a minute, that's not the van they had this morning: it's tiny, I mean just a pickup.'

Uh-oh. What's happened? We rush down.

No sweat - as we've left the bed behind for Lucia to use, everything was rattling around too much so they stopped and changed to the pickup and an estate car, driven by the son's wife. It is all safe and sound. Now it is just a question of hauling it up two flights of stairs. We all set to work.

'That's clever,' says Martin watching as they put a thick rope under the fridge and over their shoulders in a kind of fireman's lift arrangement to get it up the stairs.

'We'll have to remember that for next time.'

'Next time? We haven't even moved in here yet!'

'Maybe when we move to Belize.'

'Belize?'

'We'll talk about it later.'

'I should think so.'

Unloading takes just an hour, and after thanks and tips, they depart for the journey back to Mérida - much faster than the one over. We finally have the flat to ourselves and something to sit on at last.

We sit on the solarium, sipping a cool drink, and watching a group of schoolchildren practising formation marching over on the rough church car park. They drill and turn with great concentration in the hot evening sun.

It all seems very peaceful. But you never know.

'We'd better go and check the lamp posts', suggests Martin with a sigh.

'Now that it's Lent, maybe there won't be any dances.'

'You could still have religious rock concerts, though, that'll be allowed. Probably the way to get around it, in fact.'

'OK, but first, you must explain about Belize.'

'Well I was just having a little look on the internet.'

'That's fatal. We ought to know that by now.' He ignores me.

'And Belize looks very interesting. First, English is the main language and they have the same legal system as in the UK.'

'The Americans will be there in hordes. And *that* means the prices will be sky-high.'

'Not necessarily. I think we should take a look sometime. We can get the bus down to Chetumal and then cross over the border.'

'Probably just as well we have to go back to the UK for while. Otherwise we might get carried away again. It has been known. Plus one minor point: we don't have any money. We've only paid half for this one so far.'

Just for once, I am not the one with the mad ideas. However - Belize, that does sound intriguing. Hang on though, we have only just this minute moved in here.

So it is back to reality and a thorough check of lampposts and walls to see when the next concert is on. There are no new announcements. However, just as we are leaving *San Francisco* supermarket with some provisions we notice: a huge pile of plastic chairs.

'How come nothing is in stock when you need it? And as soon as you don't, hey presto?'

And then we call into a small clothes shop for a t-shirt and see they have a pile of sheets in a corner at the back.

Later, there is a great commotion out on the Highway. We rush to see what is going on. First come several police vans and cars, going at a stately pace, lights flashing, horns blaring. They are followed by a 4-by-4 with smoked glass windows from which banners are flapping, and then an open truck full of people in fatigues, waving flags. A couple more police cars bring up the rear.

'What's this, an invasion?'

'No: look, it's the Zapatistas' flag. Maybe it's the sub-commandante himself.'

Next day's paper confirms that Marcos came up from Chiapas to express support for indigenous craft sellers who were being threatened with eviction from their pitches within the Chichén Itzá site. Apparently the authorities say tourists have been complaining about having them all over the grounds. This seems ridiculous because no doubt there were trinket sellers there in ancient times, and with plenty of willing customers, judging by the number of offerings found down the sacred well. More like, they are undercutting the official site shops.

The convoy passes on its way and we have to get a move on to fix up caretaking and rentals for the apartment. In Playa, there are whole agencies devoted to managing holiday rentals from modest studios to huge swanky villas in Playacar where people are shelling out several thousand dollars a week and want instant attention. However, in Tulum, as they say, this market is not mature. In fact it is practically non-existent. We've found one villa for rent in Tulum pueblo and that is it. Otherwise people put up little cards on the internet café noticeboards.

We go around to a tiny real estate office just down the road. No way are we going back to the swankier place that had rubbished our apartment.

'It's a lovely apartment, right in the heart of things.'

'Absolutely.'

The young guy in the office is very interested.

'Have you many properties for rent in Tulum town?'

'No, not really.'

In fact, this is a new proposition. But looking at the building going on, it seems like Tulum will need a lettings agency pretty soon.

'You're pioneers, you guys.'

He's right there. This is not exactly a gold rush yet though. But isn't that little block of studios a few blocks off the Highway always, always full? And hasn't everyone said to us that there is nowhere to rent longer-term in Tulum - so we have a sure-fire hit on our hands?

He organises a meeting for us with the agency's founder who runs their Playa lettings operation. We sit on our balcony with her and have a big discussion.

'It's very Mexican. It's nice.'

Meaning it is definitely not the luxury gin palace you get in Playacar with designer furnishings and the latest gizmos in the kitchen, but we are not in that market. All the same, she agrees to take it on. Hooray! But we will have to hop on the bus for an hour again to Playa to stock up on some essential items that we just can't find in Tulum.

'How come we've been making do with beach towels with holes in them but our guests get lovely soft new ones?'

'Well we don't want someone posting a stinker on the blogs, do we?'

And believe me, the blogs down here are very active even outside the hurricane season. If someone gets cold coffee for breakfast, it will be out there by lunch.

We make an inventory and move all our personal stuff into the third bedroom, which we are going to lock up. This also solves the problem of buying another bed. Some time later, when we are back in the UK, Martin remembers the jars of my marmalade-chutney that he'd pushed in there at the last moment.

'What if the ants find it?'

I can see he is troubled by visions of forcing the door on our return to be greeted by ants that have gorged on the preserves and grown into monsters so that the whole room is one enormous teeming ant nest.

'Don't worry, that huge spider you saw will polish them off.'

'That's what's worrying me - what will *it* turn into?'

It is our last evening together in Tulum before we head home

It is time to have a little recap. One year on and how have we done?

'Well we now have three properties. Number one in Mérida is stuck on the market. Two has been hit by a couple of hurricanes but is doing OK, except we can't afford to stay there more than a few days. And three - we may have bought a rental property in a place where no one wants to rent. What is that saying about fortune favouring the brave?'

'Look on the bright side,' pointed out Martin, 'we got away without doing B & B.'

'I suspected that was the plan all along.'

'You know, the best thing about this year is actually *not having* any plan and just going with the flow.'

'I suppose we can always say that when we get back and people smile sympathetically and commiserate: "So it didn't quite work out then?"'

'Well I never said anything about running a B & B to anyone. I just mentioned a little property development. Now with three they think I'm a tycoon. Plus this is just phase one.'

'Also, the secret of successful business is adaptability. If it doesn't work, do something else. That's what we've done.'

'It's going to be so grey and damp back in the UK.'

'That's why we have to work hard on Plan B.'

Ah, Plan B. We'd been through so many it feels more like Plan Z now or Plan Gamma or wherever the names of hurricanes have got to this season, as they've run out of the Roman alphabet and started on the Greek.

'So what exactly does Plan B involve, apart from going back to work?'

'First we have to do something about the house back home. It's eating money.'

True, we've managed to live on around eight thousand dollars all year in Mérida. Keeping the house going in the UK has cost all of that again and then some. We'd investigated renting it out and decided the costs would wipe out any profit - plus companies, who pay the most, want a three year contract.

We need to change to something we can lock up and leave. The ideal will be to spend spring to autumn in the UK working and the winter in Mexico.

'I've seen some interesting ideas on the web.'

'Oh no, please…'

'You could do B & B for the summer.'

'Show me.'

'You'll have to wait until we're back in the UK. Best not to get carried away.'

Touché.

And suddenly it's March and we *are* back in the UK and yes, it's grey and damp. In fact, it's bloody cold. And what are we going to do now?

We have just two weeks before Martin gets absorbed back into work. However, the plan is that this won't be for more than six months. Then he'll go freelance, I'll run the B & B and we'll head out to Mexico in the winter. Then again, maybe it would be best just to bite the bullet and go back to work full-time. But that means it will be heads down for the next twenty-five years. And what is it they say about only regretting the things you don't do?

'So…these places you saw on the internet?'

'Well, I am thinking you get more for your money in the West Country.'

'There must be a reason. The part that's cheap is miles from anywhere. You know, we were spoilt in Mérida. You really can get bargains there.'

Despite this, we decide to check out Glastonbury. It seems to have the same kind of vibe as Tulum - full of craft shops and outlets selling crystals, alternative remedies and offering an amazing range of healing therapies. Instead of the Mayan ruins, it has the abbey and the Tor. This is where old and new hippies in the UK hang out. Yes, there are plenty of similarities.

'We can get a lot of synergy going with one place in Tulum and one here.'

'A lot of what?'

'I bet the volume at the Glastonbury Festival never gets anywhere near Tulum cultural centre on a regular Sunday night.'

Well it could be interesting so we go into all the estate agents to see if they have anything suitable for B & B.

There are a couple of places close to the centre but they have no parking and the spirit of peace, happiness and love to all here does not extend to free public car parks. Plus the guests - during and outside the Festival - are not likely to be high rollers *and* they will all want special vegan veggie organic breakfasts that cost a bomb in health shops.

'You know, I think it would be easier to do B & B in Mexico after all.'

'Well we could work up to that gradually.'

'So what have we been doing for the last year?'

'Market research. Now we know where we do and don't want to set up. The Caribbean coast is a much better bet. Or maybe Belize.'

When we get home, there is good and bad news from Tulum. The take up for holiday rentals is not brilliant - in fact, this being the low season, there has been one booking and that was just for two nights. Perhaps the free music had something to do with it? Never mind, there are plenty of people working in the area who want to rent long-term. So we sign a contract by email and that's that.

'There's just one thing,' says Martin. 'Now we don't have anywhere to stay long-term when we go out there.'

'Well we can always buy another place and turn it into a B & B later, once we've earned more money.'

And why not?

Chapter 18: Adios Mérida

It's July and we're heading back on the bus to Mérida. We haven't seen the house since March and will have just a couple of hours in the morning to tidy it up before heading to the notary's and handing over the keys.

We walk up from the bus station to stretch our legs after endless hours sitting on planes and buses. Stumbling along the dark streets we are out of practice with the atrocious pavements and keep on tripping.

'That's one thing I won't miss,' says Martin, pausing to mop his brow.

'And this humidity is another.'

We pass *La Flor de Santiago* - its cool interior still brightly lit at nine thirty.

We need to press on - it will have to be cheese rolls again for tonight. Just like that first night we ever spent in our house. Some things don't change.

Families are still sitting out on the pavement to get the breeze. When they nod as we go past, it feels like a goodbye.

By the time we get there, the students' cars have gone and the café has closed for the night. Although the big old house next door is sold, it still looks exactly the same; only the pale turquoise stucco is just a little more crumbled.

We scramble through the low doorway into our courtyard.

'I am just so hot', says Martin as we fumble with the lock on the front door.

Inside, we dump our bags in the empty front room and rush out to the pool and turn on the underwater light. It's the rainy season and although Lucia only moved out a couple of days ago, the water is already green.

'Pity, I was looking forward to a swim.'

I tell Martin to go up to the bedroom and put on the a/c before he passes out.

'The bed is over in the apartment - we'd better sleep there.'

The a/c in the apartment is not working. And the bed is too heavy to lug over to the house in the dark and the heat. So we settle for the hammocks we left behind for just this purpose.

'You know,' I reflect as we sit on the hammocks munching our cheese rolls in the cool blast from the a/c, 'I thought I was going to be so sad leaving this house. But now I am really feeling quite cheerful.'

'Me too,' says Martin practically asphyxiating himself with anti-mozzy spray.

There are no dogs barking that night - they probably realised they'd lost their audience and quit the neighbourhood some time ago.

We are up at six. There's no hope of a swim in the pool. The chemicals are almost out so we rush round to the pool supplies shop to get more chlorine and algaecide. I call in at the *Navidad* panificadora to buy some big round polvorone biscuits. We're already back into our regular routine.

I do a big sweep to get up as much of the dust in the house as I can while Martin doses the pool and attempts to start the lawn mower. Lucia has already warned us that it is not behaving. It refuses to cough into life. At least the grass is still green even if it is a foot high.

We will need to apologise to the new owners for quite a few things.

'Let's hope *they* don't stage a last minute withdrawal', says Martin, sounding seriously worried.

Then that's it: our agent comes to pick us up and we head off to the Notary's office for a midday signing. We begin to wish we hadn't already agreed to come back afterwards and show the new owners over the house and explain how things work - or not. But we can't leave them in the lurch - especially as our agent is taking us all out to lunch first.

So here we are back in the same office we were in less than two years ago. The ghosts of all our hopes from that steamy November seem to swirl about us. Strangely, we're really still quite cheerful. So we never got around to opening the B & B and our decorating efforts weren't going to end up in *Elle Deco*. But we had a good year and the pool's great and the garden is now a fantastic oasis and will look good again once the grass is cut.

And as Martin says: 'You should always leave something for the new owners to do.'

'Wouldn't it have been nice to keep it and add a balcony and spiral stairs down into the garden, and a colonnaded terrace and a fountain?'

'No', says Martin. 'It's nice to move on.' Then seeing my face: 'Maybe we can have those in Belize.'

The new owners are a very pleasant couple - she is Mexican and he is originally from Germany. They have both lived in the States for many years and are always making trips to Mexico to visit family members. The house is ideal for them to hold big family reunions.

Ten minutes is all it takes to sign away *La Casa del Abogado*. Then we all head off for a very convivial lunch in a famous seafood restaurant called *La Pigua* at the top of Reforma. We have to confess we've never been there despite its fame and keep quiet about the reason - *Chicken Itzá* being closer to our budget.

Then there is no putting it off. Our agent drops us at the house and we thank her for all her efforts and say well you never know - maybe one day we'll be back and buying another house in Mérida.

The new owners don't bat an eyelid when they see the grass - or the pool. They have one back in the States and know that algaecide will clear it in a couple of days. And the grass can be cut and the a/c fixed. Their teenage daughter, who is with them, looks less convinced.

We've arranged with Lucia that she'll drop by to leave the keys and say goodbye. She's branched out and is busy selling houses on the beach in the villages around Progreso so only has a few moments. We tell her we are really grateful for all the help she's given us and wish her well in her new venture and say a tearful goodbye.

Unnoticed by us, the sky has clouded over and suddenly the heavens open. We've finished showing them over the house and we're all waiting for taxis. They are going back to stay in Dan and Sofi's hotel and will be off furniture hunting tomorrow…

We ask them to say hello for us as we'd better not say goodbye: we're bound to be back staying at the hotel soon. We just might not be buying a house next time. And now we have to rush to get a bus to Cancun and then on to Akumal.

As I have my big yellow rain cape with me, I volunteer to stand in the rain to look out for the taxis. The water pouring over the road is up to my ankles. Mérida rain - I remember it well. You can't possibly cry when you are so wet already.

We say goodbye to the new owners and wish them the best - and we really mean it. They are so happy with the house we are almost envious. Now why on earth did we want to sell up?

'Maybe one day we are really going to kick ourselves for selling it.' I say as we sit damply in the taxi heading for the bus station.

'Maybe', agrees Martin. 'But as I keep on saying, unless we suddenly get global cooling, it's always going to be too darn hot.'

Good point.

www.ingramcontent.com/pod-product-compliance
Ingram Content Group UK Ltd.
Pitfield, Milton Keynes, MK11 3LW, UK
UKHW041946190726
13854UKWH00004B/1821